D0898145

Williams-Wallace International

ELUSIVE SUMMIT

Published in 1981 by
Williams-Wallace International Inc.
229 College Street
Toronto, Ontario
Canada
M5T 1R4

Copyright © 1981 Harry Henig

All rights reserved. The use of any part of this publication reproduced, transmitted in any form or by any means, electronic, mechanical, photocopy, recording or otherwise or stored in a retrieval system without prior written consent of the publisher is an infringement of the copyright law.

Canadian Cataloguing in Publication Data

Henig, Harry
  Elusive summit

Includes index.
ISBN 0-88795-014-0 (bound).   —   ISBN 0-88795-015-9 (pbk)

1. Henig, Sheila. 2. Pianist — Canada — Biography.
I. Thompson, Madeline.

ML417.H46H46   786.3'041'0924   C81-095109-6

Printed and bound in Canada.

ELUSIVE SUMMIT
THE BIOGRAPHY OF SHEILA HENIG

By
Harry Henig
and
Madeline Thompson
(Co-Author)

All research, interviews and musical material in this book was compiled by Rick Kardonne.

PUBLISHER'S NOTE:

Newspaper clippings and quotes were culled from Sheila Henig's belongings. We regret that occasionally a date of publication is missing; on those occasions we have supplied a general date. However, we felt the material was important enough to be included.

We have also used translations of European reviews which were in Sheila's possession, as the originals could not be found.

ACKNOWLEDGEMENT

We are all greatly indebted to Anne Epstein, a good friend of the Henigs, for her assistance in preparing this book for publication. Thank you Anne.

TABLE OF CONTENTS

Sheila Henig, 1958, age 24

INTRODUCTION

Over the years, I have been privileged to have known many of the greatest living musicians of our era as close friends as well as professional associates. When one travels as much as I, you do not often measure friendship with the many musicians you meet in terms of actual time spent with them, but rather the quality of the time spent with them, no matter how brief that time may be. And so, in this respect, among the most special people I have ever met was the late Canadian classical pianist Sheila Henig, who was one of the greatest musicians of our time.

There are many, many fine classical pianists in today's world. Why, among these multitudes, did Sheila rank as one of the very best? This book will explain the technical and musical reasons why. I don't have to add much more. But it was Sheila, the personality, whom I knew, about whom I wish to say a few brief words. Sheila Henig as a human being was really very special. She was a golden rarity. Sincerely generous, effusive, warm, and elegantly dignified, she exuded a purity and a goodness which is becoming increasingly rare in today's musical world. It was this warm civilized personality, expressed in her playing, together with her technical brilliance and vast musical knowledge, that made Sheila Henig, the pianist, so special.

Her passing, so suddenly, on May 15, 1979, shocked the entire musical world, both in her native Canada and abroad, where her reputation in Vienna, New York, London and other music capitals was legendary. It was soon felt that the most fitting tribute to Sheila would be to record her all-too-brief life in print so that she would never be forgotten; not only by her countless friends and admirers in the world of music but also by the general public at large — both in Canada, her home country, to whom she devoted her career, and to the whole world.

This book, therefore, is this tribute, of which I, speaking on behalf of the Canadian and international music world of which I feel so privileged to be a part, feel so honored to introduce.

MAUREEN FORRESTER

Ease the pounding of my heart
    by quieting my mind.
Steady my hurried pace.
Give me calmness amidst the
    confusion of my day.
Break the tension of my nerves
    with soothing music that lives in my memory.
Help me to know the magical restoring power
    of sleep.
Teach me the art of taking minute vacations,
    of slowing down to chat with a friend,
    To read a book
    To look at a flower.
Remind me each day of the fable of
    The Hare and the Tortoise
That I may know that there is
    more to life than speed.
Let me look upward toward the
    branches of the towering Oak
And remember that it grew great
    and strong because it grew slowly.
Slow me down Lord — Slow me down.

Anonymous

PART I
Wonder-Child

Sheila Henig, age 3½

Wonder Child

On the way to Vancouver I sat in the airplane with my hands clasped in my lap. I let my eyes swim in the vastness of the universe, my gaze lose focus, blur and grow vague in the misty immensity of space. As I was soaring high in the sky, my yearning-love for freedom made me realize my longing for rest; my yearning to seek refuge from the thronging manifold shapes of my fancy in the bosom of the simple and vast; and another yearning, opposed to my art, and perhaps for that very reason, a lure, for the unorganized, the immeasurable, the eternal — in short, for nothingness. I thought that he whose preoccupation is with excellence, longs fervently to find rest in perfection, and is not nothingness a form of perfection?

Sheila Henig, 1971

". . . she was a perfectionist in an imperfect world."

Louise Henig, 1979

Sheila would excell in her lifetime; if she believed in "destiny", and she did on occasion bring the subject up, she was on a path of almost outrageous determination to excell.

Sheila was two and a half when she was dubbed the "Shirley Temple double", but even here she exceeded her Hollywood counterpart not only charming her audience with curls and sparkling eyes, but singing, dancing, and displaying a prodigious intelligence and verbal articulateness which would, today, have educators crowing with pleasure. When offered toys and dolls for birthday presents, she point-blank refused and said — "Get me a new song". She was unequivocal in her demand that she be seen and treated as an adult. And yet, many, many times she wistfully summed herself up — "I was born old. I never was a child" — and seemed to long for the careless, undirected rummaging through childhood which most children took for granted. She would, through her whole life, tie herself to these two dichotomies and never come to peace with either of them. She would give herself strong family, hometown ties and try to soar as an artist, to be recognized in her own time, in her own place.

Born Canadian — and remaining Canadian — she had the added burden of battling her country's reluctant dragon attitude towards its own performing artists, an attitude acknowledged by many of her peers who, characteristically, are shy of defining cause and effect for fear of antagonizing what foothold they have on the Canadian arts establishment.

Winnipeg is as flat as a table top, no hills, no valleys, but if there are no extremes in the landscape, its climate makes up for it. Interestingly enough, at the time of Sheila's birth in 1934, Winnipeg was experiencing two years of climatic extremes not to be experienced again until 1977. From Edmonton to St. Louis to New York, February 1934 plummeted far below 0 farhenheit, setting record lows to this day; the following July, temperatures soared well above the 100 mark and stayed there for weeks. The weather only added to the general economic disaster which had affected North America ever since the stock market crash of 1929 broke the giddy bubble of the roaring 20s. At first glance, anyone from the inflation-plagued eighties would look at the rock-bottom prices of the era and gape in awe. The five-cent loaf of bread is a delightful anachronism, but it didn't mean much if your weekly income was five dollars, or if there was no weekly income at all. Unemployment averaged at least 25% and more in most North American cities, but this was more than just a statistic: there was no unemployment insurance, no welfare, no food stamps, just a "pitiable SOB called relief", for which huge jobless armies of all ages, both sexes (although mostly men) would stand in long lines in all kinds of weather outside government agencies — which were usually situated in the dingiest parts of town — for a tiny dole and a free bowl of soup.

It was a period of dashed dreams and resulting predictable social unrest. As hordes of unemployed men hitched rides on freight trains and travelled from coast to coast in both the U.S. and Canada, fruitlessly searching for jobs as fruit-pickers and harvesters in distant cities, they fell easy prey to radical political philosophies. Frustrated by the impotence of the still-young labour unions which were afraid to go on strike lest the few precious jobs remaining be lost, many of these unemployed men, especially in the large cities, were attracted to the red banner of the Communist party. They found common cause with a surprisingly large number of North America's most recognized intellectuals who could logically prove that the capitalist system had failed and that Russia, despite its purges and political prisons which could be conveniently ignored, represented the wave of the future. Huge May Day rallies where thousands paraded under the red banner were regularly held in New York, Toronto, Winnipeg, and many other large cities. The establishment newspapers hysterically screamed about the red Bolshevik hordes who threatened to subdue both the Stars and Stripes and the Union Jack (the Maple Leaf had not yet become the rallying point of the Canadian national conscience). But the real threat to social order came from the opposite end of the political spectrum. Far more dangerous was the shadow of the swastika. Far away in Germany, Hitler had just assumed power. While North American newspapers shrugged him off as little more than a curiosity, there was a surprisingly large group of white, gentile fifth-columnists throughout North America whose tolerance of both Blacks and Jews during the depression had snapped. Sporadic anti-Semitism, anti-Negro hate-harangues spouted from speaker's podiums and the infant invention, radio.

The average Jewish situation in Canada, and certainly the U.S., was that of a struggling working class with the fear of penury never far away and where the overpowering urge of the younger generation, instilled into them by the older generation, was to succeed via the magic channel of education in order to achieve a better, and more important, safer life.

In the early '30s, Harry Henig settled in Winnipeg where he met and married Fanny Schiffer in 1932. The Schiffer family (emigrating from Russia in the early 1900's) was highly respected in the community and across Canada. Fanny, Sheila's mother, was brought up in an Orthodox home and was imbued from childhood with the traditionalist view of Jewish morality and ethics, and this she passed on to her daughter with a gentle, deliberate intensity. She was the youngest in the family, adored music and took piano lessons for some time for her own enjoyment and the pleasure of her family. The family distinguished itself in Canada, particularly her brother, Norman, who achieved great success in his business ventures and was, at one time, a Bronfman associate. An idealist, sometime in 1926 or '27 he took his family including Fanny, to Palestine. Fanny remained with her brother for over two years and then returned to Winnipeg.

For Harry Henig, Winnipeg was one of a long line of homes, the first one being a small village in Galicia, a southern province of Poland (then part of the Austrian-Hungarian empire). From there, Henig went to the Jewish agricultural colony of Hirsch, Saskatchewan, then to New York's lower east side and finally to Winnipeg's North End. He was an amateur violinist and immediately became part of the Jewish community and culture.

The North End was a pocket — rather than a ghetto — of first-generation Jews; the normal dwelling was not the dingy red-brick tenement of the eastern cities but two-storey frame houses. More often than not they were ramshackle and ancient but they were inviting to these immigrants because they had a sense of space in comparison to the situation of being packed like sardines, one atop another, which existed in New York and Montreal. They were spotlessly clean houses, built of lumber and heated by coal or firewood. Each short block was anchored by a corner grocery store, which was often created out of the livingroom of someone's house. This Jewish community did not associate itself with poverty and they did not think of themselves as leftovers from another country; they were a cohesive, vibrant group of people maintaining a proud and culturally active communal and religious life. It shaped Sheila Henig's life beyond measure for it was here that the "performer" was nurtured; the refining of the "musician" came later, under the influence of the more English-oriented Toronto and the tutilege of Frederic Lord, where she would absorb with British-like diligence and tenacity, the techniques of her art.

Harry Henig, when he returned to Winnipeg in 1975, remembers feeling as if he was facing a new world — or rather an old world he had forgotten. "I had been liberated out of a jungle into a paradise." A feeling of serenity came over him as he saw people drive slowly, eat and talk slowly, even sleep slowly. Western people seem to have time for themselves and each other; Western hospitality is impossible to describe, much less understand. They are loyal to each other whether they know one another or not and the overall feeling is, "Live and let live". This feeling was even more so back in the 30s.

Sheila's mother, Fanny Schiffer, at age 18 — taken in Winnipeg, before leaving for Palestine.

Harry Henig, 1928, taken in Hirsch, Sask., before he married Fanny Schiffer.

Jewishness was unabashedly and proudly proclaimed all over Selkirk Avenue, called the "Jewish Uptown". There was everything available there: bakeries, delicatessens, kosher butchers and a prestigious Jewish department store which was the pride of the North End. During the depression years, however, it was a very hard life; most people lived on 25 cents a day, hoping, but not really believing, that tomorrow life would be better. It was particularly difficult to believe during the record-cold February of 1934.

The house in the middle of the block on Manitoba Avenue in the heart of Winnipeg's North End where Sheila Henig was born still stands; it was a poor-looking and dilapidated structure then, and the ensuing years have not been kind to it. An unpainted outside wooden staircase leads up to a two-room dark and gloomy attic and in February, 1934, half of that attic was occupied by Harry and Fanny Henig and their new baby, Sheila, born on the 19th. There was hardly any furniture except for an old wood stove standing in the corner of a very small kitchen, a small galvanized rusty sink nailed on to the wall supported by two metal legs. To the left of the sink there was a skimpy lumber partition which separated the one-piece toilet from the kitchen; the ceilings sloped so steeply at that point in the room the only way to get into it was to crawl on hands and knees and then back out the same way. In the second tiny room a mattress lay on the bare floor near a drapeless window which faced the street.

Those first months of Sheila's life were very difficult for the Henigs; her father remembers one night in particular. There was a raging storm outside; Sheila lay in her crib which was placed atop an orange crate near the stove, thus closest to the heat. The spark of fire smouldering in the stove was no match for the bitter cold; the walls were wet with trickles of water which froze before they reached the floor; the pipes had frozen, there was no water. Her parents were hopelessly dejected and worried as to how they could get some milk for her and keep her warm. Mr. Henig remembers that no words were necessary between him and his wife; they prayed quietly that the night would come to an end as all nights eventually do and bring a better day and a new beginning. But the night went on interminably; the agonizing noise of the howling storm could be heard inside as it raged all around the house, piling up huge snowdrifts. Walls of snow were driven along by winds of blizzard proportions. Life in the entire city had come to a halt.

But morning finally came, the winds subsided and the sun slowly rose. Neighbours came to the aid of the Henigs, bringing some milk for Sheila, a little wood for the fire. Harry didn't have a job, nothing new in those days, and finally he had to join the relief lines. In his book, *I Sold Myself a Dream*, he recounts: "The shame and bitterness can never be erased from the mind of a relief recipient. The most shameful moment of my life came when I was compelled to stand in a relief line for the first time in my life. I felt as if I were about to commit a crime. I was signing away my manhood, my pride, my self-respect — never again to feel dignity or have the courage to sit at my own table, should I ever own one, and feel that I was worthy of it."

Winter was finally over, the dark threatening snow clouds slowly broke up into small pieces of white fluff. The sun was shining again and balmy air came riding on a southern breeze and Sheila was beginning her fourth month of life. The Henigs do not remember precisely at what age Sheila began to manifest any unusualness about her; she walked very early, about six to eight months, and never crawled. She pulled herself up on the leg of a chair and reached out for a helping hand. Around this time, Harry Henig finally got a job as a Kik-Cola truck driver. In the general festivity of the event he picked Sheila up and danced around and around the tiny apartment with her celebrating the fact that she "would never be hungry again". To her parents the fact that Sheila was joyfully taking her first steps at six months of age seemed to be part and parcel of the new beginning. He swore to her that she would grow up to be a beautiful girl, she might even take dancing lessons, piano lessons, singing lessons, perhaps all three — "You might even become a star, who knows!" He vividly remembers these moments for to have a job and leave the relief line was something indeed to be celebrated and looked upon as God's blessing.

Asked if she was a fretful baby or if she cried a lot — understandable under the circumstances — he smiled and said, "No — she was just a baby in the attic". As an infant she lay in her crib always watchful, always looking, playing with her hands. He read to her from the time she was born, partly to pass the time, partly to somehow instill in her, however unconsciously, that there was a better life for her, for all of them. He would play his violin, sing songs for her, show her the music and the notes and the lyrics: in less than a year and a half Sheila was beginning to pick up the words and would sing with him. He'd show her a song once, the next time she would read it for herself. She was enormously inquisitive, interested in everything in the attic. She would sound the words out, play little word-games with her father and then begin reading the lyrics of the songs without her father's intervention. They were all the pop songs of the day — *Besame Mucho, Go To Sleep My Little Bucaroo, Old MacDonald Had a Farm, Oh Joseph, Joseph*... and a Yiddish song *Gelt* (money) saying how hard it is to be without it. Once her tongue began to form the words, she lept on the language like a streak of fire, her vocabulary increased practically by the minute.

This was a startling acceleration to the Henigs but they did not fuss, perhaps the way parents would today. In extraordinary times, extraordinary things occur and become commonplace. Instead, they simply took great pleasure in their fantastically bright vivacious baby who bounced and wriggled to music, sang along with her father in an amazing baritone voice and would cry out, "Let's dance, Daddy!" before most children could utter their first "da-da".

Before Sheila was two years old, her father had her taking the promised dancing lessons at Kelly Moore's studios. The two of them were beginning to appear at charity concerts and the like, sharing the stage as a father-daughter song and dance team, singing in both English and Yiddish and performing the little skits Mr. Henig wrote for them, with Sheila doing a solo bit as a 'speller'.

By the time she was four years old she had 200 words at her immediate disposal.

The Winnipeg press was quick to catch on:

SHEILA HENIG STAR AT JUBILEE CONCERT
Sheila Henig, aged two-and-a-half, was the star of the jubilee concert, held Sunday night in Talmud Torah Hall by the Young Mother's Association of the Talmud Torah. Little Miss Henig delighted the audience with song and dance.

Winnipeg Free Press, Jan. 28, 1937

She was quick to memorize songs that her father brought for her. When asked what type of toy she wanted, she would reply always: "I don't want toys. I am not a baby. I want a new song. I want 'Go To Sleep My Little Buckaroo'." And she would further insist that in order to sing properly she had to have a piano.

"My dear child," her father replied, "how can I possibly get you a piano? Even an old one would cost around twenty dollars. We just don't have the money and besides, if we were to bring a piano into the attic, the floor would probably collapse."

"Then promise me you'll buy one just as soon as you have enough money," Sheila insisted.

Trying to do his best, Harry Henig made her a "pretend" piano. He took a piece of rope and tied up two pieces of wood one each end, hung it over the side of her crib, and made it appear as piano pedals. She would crawl inside her crib, put her feet through, reach to the pieces of wood and sing, pretending she was playing by making piano-playing motions with her fingers and manipulating the pieces of wood with her feet. That ingenious invention kept her happy for the time being.

It was becoming more and more evident that Sheila was not an ordinary child: she was a child with a very high I.Q., perhaps a genius, who loved music. She also had a willful, high-profile personality and she was not shy of displaying it. Her father recalls an incident which happened when she was just two years old. He had read an article in a Winnipeg newspaper which stated a radio station was inviting contestants of three years and up to be brought down to the studio by their parents to audition for a singing concert. Sheila's mother took her downtown for an audition and she was accepted (obviously, they were prepared to ignore the age limit). A few days before the contest, Mr. Henig took her to the studio several times for rehearsal with the piano accompanist. Sheila was ready, relaxed, and sang like a trooper. However, as often happens, there was the unpredictable element: on the day of the contest they found to their dismay that the original accompanist had taken ill and there was a substitute. Sheila reverted to being a two-year-old — of sorts — became quite nervous about the change and lost the contest. On the way home she hugged her father and cried bitterly, repeating over and over again: "Daddy! I'm sorry! I'll never lose again. I promise!" The incident happened two months after her second birthday.

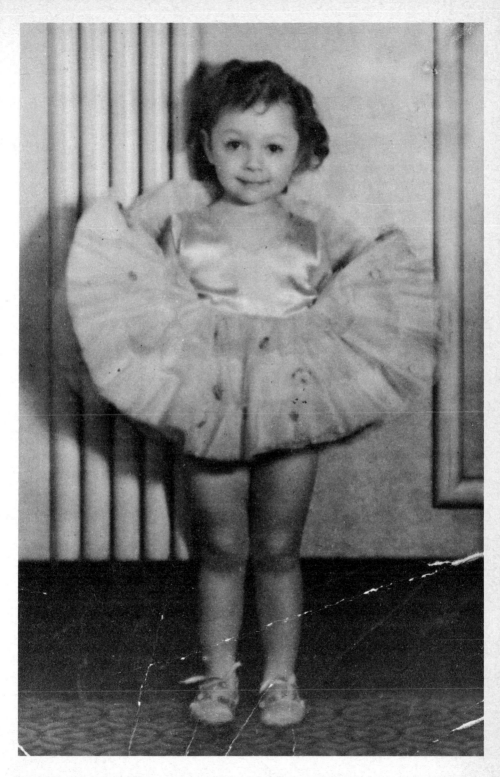

Sheila, snapped just before the Jubilee Concert performance.

It was no great loss, for invitations were pouring in from charitable organizations asking Sheila to appear on stage as a singer-tap-dancer. She was actually announced in the press as, "Sheila Henig, baby singer and dancer". She would be terrified backstage of the dark shadows which lurked about her as she waited in the wings for her cue, but when it came, she would put on the performer's smile and make her entrance.

Sheila's parents were very happy with her accomplishments: in those days, which were before the heyday of the child psychologist and all the 'how-to' books on child-raising, children were more apt to be considered 'little people' and were left to pursue their talents as they erupted. So when Sheila signed her first professional singing contract at the age of three and a bit, the neighbours didn't jump on the Henigs back and warn them of "exploitation"; no one shook their finger at them and talked of the beauties of 'natural' childhood. First and foremost, Sheila thrived on the stage exposure and the chance to perform; she had never played with children her own age and didn't seem to miss that kind of life. She was a glowing, vivacious little girl, who knew she was well-loved, and everybody delighted in her; any harmful effects were not immediately forthcoming. Later she seemed to feel very keenly that she had missed out on something important, but at the time, she was totally at ease in the limelight.

The Beacon Theatre on Winnipeg's Main Street specialized in live stage shows in between regular movie features. They were interested in Sheila. After a few meetings with the management her father, in the presence of Sheila, signed her first contract in the entertainment world: she would receive twenty dollars for three performances a day, for seven days.

Her entertainment horizon was growing by leaps and bounds; she was becoming very popular, often referred to as 'The Midget', and she had Winnipeg buzzing. In music circles she was considered a child prodigy which, considering everything, was probably an understatement. After her first seven-day stint at the Beacon, she was signed a few weeks later to another seven-day contract. Her appearances were publicized widely through the Winnipeg newspapers:

CHILD WONDER IS BIG ATTRACTION AT BEACON STAGE SHOW.
A baby girl from the North End, Sheila Henig, is a veritable sensation at the Beacon Theatre. She amazes the audience by the proficiency with which she spells words that would puzzle her elders; names the capitals of various countries and displays much other knowledge unusual in one so young. Sheila's song is a hit with her audience and when she follows it with a smart tap dance she just about stops the show. She is to be seen in evening performances only.
                    Winnipeg Tribune, Monday, April 25, 1938.

For curiosity's sake, the features showing at this particular week's performances were, "The Prisoner of Zenda", starring Ronald Coleman, and

"Lifers of the Party", a comedy (Sunday, Monday and Tuesday); for the remainder of the week, Mary Boland was starring in "Marry the Girl" and Miriam Hopkins in "Men Are Not Gods". Sheila's co-stars in the stage talent department included a dance team from Toledo, Dorethea LaDorr and Enrico Pasquale who performed "colourful presentations of the modern dances"; Eddie Stone, a novelty instrumentalist of "distinctly high class"; someone named Walt billed as a "wizard of the accordian", Alex Johnston, a well-known baritone and Shirley Bush with songs and dances. The live entertainment was rounded out by an emcee (in this case, a mistress of ceremonies) and the Beacon Band in the pit.

Sheila's public appearances in Winnipeg were interrupted for a period, but her popularity — that is, her press notices — increased, if anything. The Henigs were evicted from their attic home of four years and the parents felt it was as good a time as any to make the trek to Los Angeles — "baby Henig" was already being compared to her famous counterpart, Shirley Temple. Harry Henig would stay back in Winnipeg, keeping his job as a Kik-Cola driver and Fanny would take Sheila to visit her sister in Los Angeles. The day before they were to depart, Sheila came down with a cold and the journey was postponed for a few days. A local reporter took the opportunity to interview her in her room, for she was confined to her crib until the cold passed. J.C. Royle's published interview gives us perhaps the most complete picture of Sheila's 'public personna' at the time:

> **SHEILA, AGED 4, HOPES THAT FILMS NEED BRAINS**
> Tot, Who Can Dance, Sing, Read, Write And Spell Is Heading For Hollywood.
> Mr. and Mrs. Harry Henig's Sheila is a mighty smart little tot — and pretty, too. Her eyes are as big and as glistening brown as ripe chestnuts. Her sweet bit of round face with transparent complexion and uptilted nose is crowned by a mass of kinky curls that fall down all round her dark brown crown, even (if they are not pushed frequently out of the way with a graceful flick of a small hand) over her forehead.
> And she can sing in English and in Jewish, can tap dance, perform acrobatics and toe dance, can spell nearly 200 words, read, write some, and can add and subtract. Having only just reached the colossal (to her) age of four years she may be called by that horrible name given to bright and charming little beings, "child prodigy".

J.C. Royle went on to describe the parents pride in their youngster, how they scrimped and saved every cent to hire the best singing and dancing teachers available in Winnipeg to teach the child. Then he got into the 'meat' of the interview.

Sheila, clad in a sleeping suit, leaned on the railing of her crib and sang to herself in her piping voice (a trifle husky, for she had caught a cold) when a Tribune reporter visited her Monday. A neighbour woman had called the Tribune to tell of the wonderful things the child could do.

She could not sing — not well enough for a visitor — with her sore throat, she insisted. She was not dressed for dancing. So she confined herself to academic accomplishments.

She spelled "Mississippi river" correctly without hesitation (Have I got it right?) then went on to "Manitoba", "Winnipeg", "Hollywood" and plenty of other words. In the intervals Mrs. Henig drew out a dozen or more songs. Sheila sings "Bei Mir Bist du Schoen", "When The Organ Played O Promise Me" and "Wie Shlecht Es Is Ohn Gelt" (which her mother maintained she sings with wonderful feeling in Jewish), to mention but a few.

Then she showed how well she could write. All she needs to do, so said her mother, is to see a word once, and she can spell it and write it.

Winnipeg Tribune, April 1938.

Sheila willingly posed for her picture until the flash discharge made her "see all white and brown" then she dug her heels in and refused any more pictures until cajoling and bribes appeased her. The reporter made an appointment to re-photograph her on the day of departure and moments before Sheila and her mother boarded the train, he took the published photograph of her in the train station, dictionary in front of her, all sparkling eyes and laughter. She was, indeed, a charmer.

As usual, when her father offered to buy her a toy to take with her, she refused. "I really don't want toys. I would rather you get me a new song." He did, however, buy her a doll, something she could cuddle and hold on to during the long journey. And she was very happy with it.

As the train was puffing along, a reporter from the Philadelphia Inquirer, who was sitting across the aisle from Sheila and her mother, engaged her in a conversation and was tremendously impressed. He asked her mother for a photograph of the child but all she could offer him was the one which would appear in the Winnipeg newspapers shortly. He used it, and Sheila thus received her first exposure in the American press. It was captioned, "*CANADA HAS A STARLET: WINNIPEG'S WONDER CHILD IS GOING TO HOLLYWOOD. If Hollywood needs brains, then four-year-old Sheila Henig is going places.*" The article continued in much the same vein as the others had: listing her accomplishments, remarking on the glowing pride her parents took in her, and never failing to describe the big brown eyes, the mass of curls, and the smile that looked like a giggle sounded.

It was the Golden Era of Hollywood. Sheila was going to be in Los Angeles for at least six months and her mother was in no hurry to push her through the studio treadmill. Eddie Cantor was a close friend of Sheila's Aunt

The Philadelphia

PUBLIC 🎀 LEDGER

Entered as second-class matter,
Postoffice, Philadelphia

PHILADELPHIA, SUNDAY MORNING, APRIL

1938

Inquirer C

Canada Has a Starlet

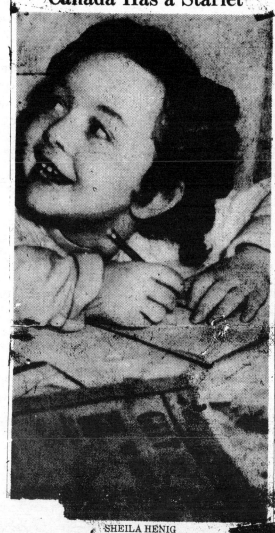

SHEILA HENIG

Goldie and he got to know the child shortly after their arrival. His advice was unequivocal: let her grow up as normally as possible; don't make a movie star out of her. It was sound advice, which Mrs. Henig and her sister listened to. Sheila did appear on radio, in repeated performances on the International Jewish Hour and on hearing her and seeing her perform, there was no question in Cantor's mind that she was destined to become an international artist "of some flavour". The question was, of her many talents which would she concentrate on, would she use them all or discover something new. She was only four years old and much too young for that kind of decision to be made. Although she created a stir in Hollywood the pressure to push her to the top was restrained and for the most part, she lived as normal a childhood life there as she would ever experience again. As usual, the press covered her radio performances both at home and locally, in Los Angeles.

WONDER CHILD ON JEWISH INTERNATIONAL HOUR

Winnipeg's wonder child is delighting the audience of the Jewish International Hour, during her repeated appearances over the program. Little four-year-old Sheila Henig, daughter of Mr. and Mrs. Harry Henig of Winnipeg, Canada, is a beautiful child, possessing unusual talent in singing, both English and Jewish; dancing; writing; reading; and can she spell! Sheila will spell without hesitation, the longest and most difficult words, upon request.

Winnipeg's wonder child is certainly a good bet for the movies . . . she's full of beauty, charm, and personality . . . and you'll probably be seeing her on the screen one of these days. In the meantime . . . listen to her over The Jewish International Broadcasting Hour.

(a Los Angeles newspaper, Summer of 1938)

Sheila and her father were very close during these early years primarily because they had performed together and there is a special bond between stage partners. She wrote him many letters from Los Angeles, not all of which he's kept, but they were always touching communications, full of innocence and simplicity, and to him they are priceless.

October 12, 1938
Dear Daddy,
Aunt Goldie is very nice to Mommy and me. I think she likes us very much. She also bought me a doll from a man on the beach. Now I have two dolls and love them both, especially the one you bought me when we were leaving Winnipeg. Yesterday Mommy took me to see Eddie Cantor. I sang for him. He said that he liked me very much. He kissed me on my forehead and smiled. On the way back we walked up a very high stairs and just then, a big fat man brushed past me and knocked my dolly's head off. It rolled all the way down to the street. Mommy had to run all the way down to pick it up. I hope it doesn't fall off again. I miss you, Daddy, and wish I were back home with you. Please write to Mommy and me, and tell us that we

can come home. I cry when I think of the times you and I sang songs together, which we enjoyed very much. I wish that we can do it again real soon. Mommy promised me that we will be going back home by the end of the year. I am hoping that she'll keep her promise.

With love,
Sheila.

Oh! I almost forgot to tell you. I'll be singing on the radio tomorrow night. Remember to listen in. I love you! Sheila.

Four months after Sheila returned to Winnipeg, she was back on stage again. Her reviews were more effusive than ever, as if her hometown recognized that even if she hadn't become a movie star, she had the approval of the land of magic.

LITTLE SONGSTRESS DELIGHTS AUDIENCE AT DANCE REVIEW.

In well nigh breathless amazement, a crowded audience at the Dominion Theatre, Thursday evening, stood and heard a little girl, Sheila Henig, newly up from Hollywood, sing the opening song at the annual revue by the dance pupils of Arthur Scott and Doreen Ward. The child is a skilled stage artist, without the slightest sign of self-consciousness, and she stopped the show cold, right there and then. The song, A Salute to Their Majesties, simply God Save The King, was delivered with such art and patriotic feeling rarely heard on local stages.

Winnipeg Tribune, May 4, 1939

Two years later, in the thick of world war II when the fate of the Allies seemed very bleak indeed, the Henigs moved into a two-room downstairs apartment consisting of a very small kitchen and a convertible bedroom-living room, still in Winnipeg's North End. Gordon Kushner, a young, talented pianist, was living with his parents directly across the street. He was her first piano teacher. Sheila was just under six.

Gordon Kushner, and later, Sheila, were only two of the internationally known musicians and entertainment personalities to come out of Winnipeg in the 30s and 40s. Others who grew up in the predominantly Jewish North End were the acclaimed cellists Zara Nelsova and Isaac Mamott, and one of Canada's leading string musicians, John Waterhouse. Then there was Arnold Spohr, director of the Royal Winnipeg Ballet for many years — to say nothing of the Ballet itself. In the more popular entertainment category Winnipeg gave birth to and nurtured David Steinberg, and America's most popular game show host, "Let's Make a Deal" Monty Hall. And there were many more. It is not the purpose of this book to outline "why", but simply to point out an interesting phenomenon that Winnipeg could hold its own in cultural output with Chicago, a city eight times its size. Certainly, in the 20s and 30s, Winnipeg was a hotbed of radical, socialist intellectual activity, at one time the communist centre of

Canada in the days when Communism was an idealistic social-political philosophy. In the 30s and 40s when the world was held in the grip of Hitlerism, the Jewish community in Winnipeg intensely nourished their religious and cultural heritage. The rich Eastern European cantorial tradition in which the cantors who led the prayer services usually had a formal classical and romantic operatic background, continued in Winnipeg while it was being snuffed out elsewhere.

All this is by way of setting the scene in which Sheila Henig began her career as a classical pianist. The move to the ground-floor flat meant that when the money was available, they could at least accommodate a piano. Gordon Kushner, at that time an established concert pianist, was giving concerts at the Men's Musical Club (on Broadway in downtown Winnipeg) and the Celebrity Concert Series. Today he is Vice President of Toronto's Royal Conservatory of Music. Kushner had a reputation as a quick-learning, accurate and emotionally sensitive pianist. There were some CBC broadcasts as well; then, as well as now, local talent was underpaid and underpromoted in comparison to the numerous visiting performers who had a "name" reputation acquired elsewhere (no matter how obscure that reputation might actually be "elsewhere."), but the exposure did him no harm. There were thousands of little girls and boys taking piano lessons from hundreds of teachers across Canada; how amazing are the machinations of fate that it should be a musician of Kushner's calibre giving Sheila her first lessons. She studied with him for only a year but Kushner to this day can remember no pupil who was as bright, or who learned as quickly as she did.

The piano lessons seemed to signal to Sheila that it was time to put her formidable intelligence and drive to concentrated purpose — to be a great pianist was not a five-year-old's fantasy but a driving ambition for her, one which she pursued with unrelenting dedication. The influence of the Jewish milieu spurred her on, there is no question — her grandfather arrived at the apartment weekly to teach her Yiddish and she had been surrounded with the Jewish reverence for the arts in general, and music in particular. She was the one who demanded piano lessons, continued dance lessons, and as many public appearances as she could get. More and more her parents vascilated on the sidelines, both trying to stay out of her way and trying to help her through as normal a childhood as they could get her to accept. Understandably, they took great pride in her achievements and could not help but marvel at this little person they had brought into the world. For them it was a dilemma that couldn't be solved: wanting to push her on in her chosen path and wanting to treat her as a child. Again, in the Jewish tradition, they accepted what fate had put in front of them.

As Sheila was racing through her first John Williams books — the first one in three weeks, the second and third as quickly — she also began school. She was just under the age of six but it seemed the appropriate thing to do. It might be expected that with her fiery determination to be a concert pianist she would ignore her school work except to put in the hours required. Instead, she excelled. Academically, she repeated the same pattern as she did with her piano studies — she was in grade 3 by the time the first school year was over. No one can remember precisely how long she remained in grade one, but her father, with a smile and a shrug of his shoulders, remarks: "She could read and write, you know, when she started. I know within a week she was running around to all the other kids in her class showing them how to do their work. Without meaning to be cheeky or brash, she was taking over for the teacher. They didn't know what to do with her." This last is probably a major understatement — no one at that time had done any 'studies', or understood very well the phenomenon of the child prodigy; they were considered by the polite as "peculiarities", and by the not-so-polite, including most other children, as "freaks of nature".

Her rapid advance through the grades in her first year caused some problems. In no time at all she was amongst children two and three years older than herself and they didn't know what to do with her either. In the manner of children everywhere, they gave her a hard time. Because she was, as she remarked later, "born an adult", she looked like a six-year-old but socialized and behaved, to all intents and purposes, much older than her schoolmates. It was not that they didn't like her per se, but almost everything about her set her apart from her peers. Her command of the language and her unnatural (for a child) dedication to a piano career put her in the behavoural league of individuals much her senior.

It was during the winter of her first year of school that Mr. Henig was looking through a newspaper and the 'Personal' column caught his attention. A father had inserted an ad for his young daughter.

My daughter Carol is twelve years old and very lonely. She would welcome a penpal who would be interested to write to her. We live on a farm near Calgary, Alberta. Write to Carol Brenner: Box 36X.

Sheila's father showed it to Sheila and she jumped at the idea of corresponding with Carol.

Feb. 22, 1940
Dear Carol:
   I have just read a newspaper clipping in which your father is seeking a penpal for you. I would be very happy to correspond with you if you'll agree.
   Let's try to get to know each other by exchanging a few letters. Perhaps it will lead to mutual interest and friendship. I must warn you, however, that I have a lot to write about. Should you find that my letters do not interest you, please tell me so. I'll understand. I would like to be your friend, and write to you as often as time will permit me. I have much to tell you. It'll probably take a year or more

to bring you up to date before I begin relating on present events. I am ecstatic about having a friend way out West and I am hoping that you'll feel the same.

Your penpal,
Sheila

March 20, 1940
Dear Sheila:

Thanks a million for taking the time to write to me. Your letter seems to indicate that you are a very nice girl. However, you didn't mention your age. Reading your letter I decided to ask you how old you are. Are you about my age or quite a bit older? It's important for me to know. I'm twelve years old. I am hoping that you'll answer my question in your next letter.

Your penpal,
Carol.

These letters were obviously going to be a welcome bit of friendship in Sheila's life. By the time the winter was over Sheila's first year in school had seen more harrassment than most six-years-olds had to cope with. Her uncle had made a little fur coat for her (oppossum); her father can remember Sheila coming home every day with it hanging in strips, Sheila sobbing. Her schoolmates had torn it to shreds. Fanny Henig would diligently sew it back together for the coat was of great practical value — Winnipeg winters were, and are, notably cold, and she and Harry would not easily forget the dismal first few months of Sheila's life. Every day she wore the coat and every night her mother sewed it back together again until, gratefully for both of them, the winter ended and Sheila had outgrown it.

April 12, 1940
Dear Carol:

In answer to your inquiry about my age, I am six years old — I go to school and am doing very well. I wish to reassure you though, that the difference in our age should not be a problem to our friendship. I was transferred to grade three only a few weeks ago, which has created a bit of difficulty for me. I have hardly any friends, since the kids in the entire class are a few years older than I. I had my birthday party on February 19th. We had a lovely time and a lot of fun. There were a few girls and two boys with whom I am quite friendly and the age difference didn't seem to bother them. My Daddy bought me a new sheet of music; a song called "One Night When the Moon Was so Mellow, Rosita Met Young Manuello". It's a very nice song. I love it. He also brought a little puppy home for me and I call him Tiger. You should see how cute he is. He is black. Only his paws, face and ears are white. He has a tiny pink nose, and when I cuddle him in my arms he keeps on licking my *face. He is only two weeks old, but he knows how to lick his milk from a bowl. I love animals, don't you? He sleeps with me in my bed at night, tucked in under the covers. During the night I can sometimes feel him licking my face. I hug him and he falls asleep again. My Mommy is a bit angry with me on occasion. She claims that I am wasting too much time with Tiger. I do, however, manage to do quite well in school. I sometimes feel that I want to act like a child, although I don't remember ever being one. I must have been born old, which is probably my own fault. I am obsessed with an ambition to become a concert pianist someday. In order to accomplish this, one must act and feel old. This feeling of course isn't new to me. I have been performing on stage since I was two years old. I do, however, get an urge once in a while to act a bit childish just for the fun of it. I sometimes envy other kids of my age. They are free. They have no ambitions. They attend school, and act like third graders should. I hope I am not boring you with my silly stories and my somewhat serious older outlook. Hoping to hear from you soon.*

Sheila.

To say that Sheila was friendless would be an error; she had girlfriends and would occasionally invite them home after school. Her father recalls that she would try to get into their world but she was never interested in the things that her girlfriends wanted to do. Invariably Sheila would take on the role of teacher and leader, organizing the games they would play which always had a 'performance' cast to them. They would not be games of running and jumping, hide and seek, or clowning about making faces, but rather play-acting games about "real" things. Sheila couldn't play the clown, couldn't throw herself around as kids do and be silly. "She was never, never silly. I cannot ever recall her making faces, pretending she was a bird, 'falling down dead', anything like that," her father remarked. "To us — and I guess, our neighbours and friends — she was always great fun to have around because she was so vivacious and imaginative, so bright. She was such an enjoyable person to have in the house that we forgot she was a child."

August 18, 1940
Dear Sheila:
   You write the most interesting letters. I find it hard to believe that you are only six-and-a-half years old. My father read your last letter, and he too was amazed how articulate and intelligent you are. He told me to ask you for a photograph of yourself, so that we can satisfy our curiosity as to your age.
   Here is something I hadn't mentioned in my first letter. I simply didn't have the courage to tell you then. I was involved in an accident about two years ago. It happened on our farm not far from the house. My brother Scott was driving a team of horses hitched to a wagon. I was running, trying to get

a ride when I tripped on a piece of wood, and one wheel rolled over me. I didn't feel that I was hurt until my parents helped me get up. I fell down again, because my right leg and arm were numb. My father drove me to a hospital in Calgary where I was confined to a wheelchair, and I had to undergo special exercises for two months. The use of my limbs has not completely been restored; however I manage to get around in a wheelchair most of the time, hoping and waiting for a miracle to happen so that I can walk again. Now that you know my problem I hope that you don't begin feeling sorry for me, because that would be very painful to accept.

Your friend,
Carol

P.S. Just in case you are wondering how I manage to write, don't. My brother Scot writes all my letters. Carol.
PPS I'm hoping that I'll be able to go to Calgary one day when I am better and manage to take a photograph of myself. Then I'll mail it on to you.

Carol

Time was passing fast for Sheila. She was taking piano lessons, singing lessons, dancing lessons. She performed occasionally — recitals and charity concerts — and she practiced, practiced, practiced, the piano. She no longer pursued the stardom she knew as a two-and-a-half year old. She had put those years behind as solidly as she now pursued excellence as a musician. She had her own piano now, at the cost of thirty dollars, and she was obsessed that she would one day become a concert pianist; the obsession was no pipe dream for she was blessed with an incredible memory. While the other children were playing outdoors in the lovely summer weather, she was inside, practicing for hours, always reaching for perfection and the gold star at the end of every lesson.

The Henigs had managed to save up two hundred dollars and made a down-payment on a nineteen-hundred-dollar cottage on Magnus Avenue and McGregor Street. It looked like a Japanese hut. The roof was black and very low; the outside walls were covered with dark grey stucco mixed with ground-up glistening stones which sparkled like bits of diamonds against the sun. The doors and windows were kept tightly shut to keep out the slightest noise which might distract Sheila's concentration while she was practising.

Even though she wasn't receiving any replies, she kept writing to Carol. Finally, on a bright sunny day in July, 1941, she came running excitedly into the house with a letter in her hand.

July 2, 1941
Dear Sheila,
Please accept my apologies for not writing sooner. For almost a year I have been undergoing painful physical therapy again, and I had surgery done several times to my leg and arm. I'm happy to inform you that I am feeling much better now though I still don't have the full use of them. I'm

now able, with difficulty, of course, to write my own letters. What do you think of my scribbling? It looks great to me. My brother drives me to school by horse and buggy each day. We take my wheelchair with us and I use it when I get tired. The one-room country school is about a mile north of us. It's the kind you see in picture books and it is just as pretty when the snow is piled up around it. It's red, too. I have adjusted to my awkward way of life knowing that my physical disability can't completely be corrected. My mother keeps reassuring me that I'll grow out of it, but I know that it's only wishful thinking on her part, and of course she's trying to make me feel better.

Your friend
Carol.

Sheila answered her in a way that may or may not have been any consolation to Carol, but she indicated some of her own longing for a more natural, spontaneous lifestyle. . . . *I want you to believe me when I say that I think you are a very lucky girl. You have parents who love you and a brother who gives you assistance when you need it. You probably own horses, cows, chickens, a dog, and a cat or two. You are surrounded by animals that I love very much: I am sure you do too. You are living on a farm where you see spring gradually reappearing out of the depth of winter. You see trees blossoming and coming into full bloom. You watch the grass each day getting greener.*

You are a nature child which I'll probably never be. All of these things should be of some comfort to you.

She mentioned they had moved to a new house. *Although it's very small, it is much more comfortable than the dark, cold attic where we lived before. I remember my parents chopping wood in the backyard when heavy snow was falling and I was hoping that it would stop. Otherwise my Mom would have to carry me on her back for my singing lesson because I was too little to walk in the snow.*

By her own design, Sheila's life was so organized that spontaneity was out of the picture, but that was the way she wanted it. She never had an opportunity of being involved in athletic activities — either individual or team sports — for fear she would get hurt and then she wouldn't be able to play the piano; she might catch a cold and she couldn't sing. Her parents went along with her on this; Mrs. Henig would watch her like a hawk — "Sheila, watch it, don't catch a cold, your lesson's tomorrow. If you catch a cold your lesson will be down the drain."

With her native maturity and adult perceptions, Sheila was very aware that every lesson she took was a drain on the family's finances. While her parents didn't want the rigid disciplined life for her, they nevertheless had to live with the reality of her. Neither they, nor anyone who knew her, could resist her tremendous vitality — "so small and yet there was more life in her little finger than most have in their whole body", was the general view of Sheila by neighbours and relatives. She took dramatic classes when she was about seven for a while and she'd race in the door of their home and want to immediately play all the dramatic scenes with her father. She had always expressed herself in this way; she loved the outpouring of energy afforded to her when she would play through her scenes and was never self-conscious about 'performing' in the living-room of her home — to her it was not a performance at all but simply an extension of her own energy. If she was serious about her work, she was impish in her behaviour around adults; her sense of humour was one of intelligence and subtlety.

Sheila was not impervious to the world of events outside her own small world of music. Her father, while driving his Kik-Cola truck, accidentally killed a three-year-old boy; the child, a deaf-mute, had tumbled out of the back of a milk truck directly into Mr. Henig's path. He was killed instantly. The trauma put Mr. Henig to bed for a week, but it sent Sheila into emotional eruptions for weeks. Her schoolmates accused her father of being a "killer" and it took endless gentle explanations from Fanny Henig to make Sheila understand how it happened — it was an accident. After a week, Mr. Henig was back driving again — a very difficult experience, one he remembers to this day — but Sheila would still break out into uncontrollable sobs, three and four weeks later — "The poor child is dead!" — and Fanny would once more have to try and explain the situation, the nature of accidents and the precariousness of life itself. For several weeks Sheila wouldn't go to school at all, for her schoolmates were still harrassing her about the incident. The Henigs finally moved to a new neighbourhood to end the situation.

Sheila and Carol continued to correspond sporadically, not from lack of enthusiasm for each other and their growing penpal friendship but because both of them were caught up in intense experiences, each in their own world. It is difficult to say precisely how Carol's emotional and social life was developing but it appeared to be running what was considered to be a normal course. For Sheila, Carol represented the closest companion she had to whom she could unburden herself and talk about feelings and changes in her life and her only close link with a 'normalized' existence; this need either she couldn't, or wouldn't fulfill in her everyday surroundings. In February of 1943 Carol wrote her again saying she was finally on the mend and optimism was in the air, and this made Sheila very happy indeed. Carol also thanked her for the picture she sent — "Your compassionate letters and your expressive face project much love, personality and kindness. I am mighty proud of having the privilege of corresponding with you . . . " Then she added a bit of "girlish gossip" — "I have a boyfriend. His name is Peter. He, too, lives on a farm with his parents. Yesterday, I promised him that when I sufficiently recover and walk without the support of a cane, I'll go with him to a movie in Calgary. That's a good reason for me to get better quickly. I am beginning to like boys. Don't you?"

Sheila's answering letter is lost but "liking boys" was not a question she could answer yet. She wrote Carol regularly although she went long periods without a reply. The pressure to excell as a pianist was growing each day in her but in spite of her overloaded schedule she embarked on a new venture in July and August of 1943. She wrote a play with music, gathered up every kid in the block and began rehearsing it in a dilapidated old garage at the rear of the Henig house. She was the authoress, director, set and costume designer, and leading performer, an outpouring of creativity, rather than megalomania, which had all the neighbours gasping and the kids eating out of her hand. When Sheila was in her own milieu and could pour out her energy unhindered by the restrictions of lessons and the need to achieve to others' standards, she could manage even the most recalcitrant children beautifully. She had them all helping her, decorating the makeshift stage with crepe paper; she coached them in their roles and had them moving about the stage like professionals. They sold tickets from door to door and the entire neighbourhood turned out to see the play, netting a generous sum of money which the kids gave to a charitable organization.

In this last home before they left Winnipeg, Sheila seemed to be more a part of the neighbourhood community. An English couple lived next door to them, with a daughter twelve, and a son, Billy, ten. They were nice, friendly people who loved Sheila and invited her over often to play with their children.

"She came home one day," Mr. Henig recalls, "and said Billy was paralyzed from the waist down — we found out he'd had polio which had left him crippled and he couldn't walk." He remembers that Sheila spent more and more time with Billy, to the point of neglecting her piano studies — "Something extraordinary for her," he recounts.

"I decided to talk to her about it. I was very moved by her reply — as always she made it very clear she would make up her own mind about these things.

" 'Daddy,' she remarked, 'Billy is crippled, he can't walk, and I feel very sorry for him. I read to him, teach him spelling and writing, somebody has to help him. And besides, he's always very happy to see me.'

"This, I think, was the only time in her young life when something besides music took precedence over the piano."

Sheila was precocious, but she was also a lovable child who adored her parents; well-known throughout Winnipeg as an entertainer, people had nothing but praise for her as a human being, for her bubbling personality and compassionate nature. People generally saw only this bright, gifted side of her.

October 28, 1943
Dear Carol:

Last week I had a very traumatic experience which is still haunting me, especially at night. When I expect my dog Tiger to jump into my bed, when I go to sleep, he isn't there. A few days ago I walked out of our yard and forgot to shut the gate. Tiger apparently tried to follow me. He walked onto the street and was killed by a passing car. I heard brakes screeching behind me, ran back a block and found my Tiger lying in a pool of blood. I screamed and my mother came running out of the house. We picked up the bundle of fluff and carried him into the kitchen, but he was dead! I somehow haven't been the same since. I cry a lot, because my lovable Tiger is gone. My father came home for lunch and found me and my Mom crying. He tried to calm us down, promising to bring me another puppy, but I refused and kept crying. I didn't go to school for several days until my parents coaxed me into going back.

My father told me, "Crying isn't going to help, Tiger will not come back. I know it's a very painful experience, I too feel very badly. I liked the little rascal, but that's the way life is." I found some consolation in his words, although I didn't exactly know what it meant.

I should however, consider myself lucky that this happened after my piano exams. Had it happened before I would have probably flunked. I don't think that there is another puppy around that's as cute as my Tiger was, and I don't intend to get another one and perhaps have to go through it all again.

I have no other important news at the moment. I attend school as usual, and envy the kids who participate in all sorts of sports, especially when snow begins to fall. I'm living a very protected life which excludes sports activities, or rolling around in the snow, just in case I catch a cold that would mean missing more singing lessons. I can't join my class in skating because I might fall and hurt my finger, hand or arm and that would interfere with my piano playing. My gym teacher was very persistant that I take part in all activities until my mother had our family doctor write a letter saying that I'm to be excused from the gym class and swimming. I keep slaving away at the piano day after day. Slaving is perhaps the wrong word, although it's just that. To me it has a different meaning, because I love it. When I practice a score and reach a point that I feel comfortable playing it, I then work on phrasing and interpretation. I put my heart and soul into it until it becomes a part of me. And, after weeks of practice, I actually begin enjoying it. I have then reached a stage where I can express myself musically through my fingers, which to me is so exciting and gratifying. Everything has its price, I suppose, and I'm not about to expose myself to any risk of getting into trouble even if it's only for a day. "Stay away from snow, ice, water", that's what my teachers preach.

I hope you don't get bored reading this silly letter. I just wanted to get it off my chest.

Looking forward to hearing from you.

Sheila.

In August of 1944, family problems uprooted the Henigs. Fanny Henig's sister, recently widowed, needed someone to help operate her store in

Brantford, Ontario. Harry Henig, who still worked as Kik-Cola driver, was finding that lugging cases of pop was becoming too hard on his slight frame. It had reached the point, a couple of weeks before, when he had just up and quit his job. Although it meant uprooting Sheila from all she knew in Winnipeg and her strict schedule of music and dance lessons, a move to the central part of Canada where the music environment was perhaps more sophisticated, certainly more eclectic, would probably be good for her. Her only intimate friend was a penpal so there was no trauma in cutting her social ties. She lamented only leaving Billy — "The other kids don't care," she worried.

Sheila was ten and a half, and at this point, she had a six-month-old baby sister, Louise, upon whom she showered all the love that had been given to her puppy, Tiger. There was no sibling jealousies involved because of the age difference and because by the time of the advent of Louise, Sheila already had a firmly established 'identity'. She cuddled the infant in her arms and occasionally, when she thought no one was looking, would try to make her tiny fingers play the piano. If anything, their sisterhood was to have a detrimental effect on Louise rather than Sheila.

Their stay in Brantford turned out to be little more than a stopover, for six months later they moved to Toronto where Sheila could study at the Royal Conservatory of Music. Brief as it was, her residence in this small city in Ontario was of immeasurable importance to her musically, for she studied with Frederic Lord, who embodied the British tradition of stylistic conventions, rounding out the early influence of the Jewish heritage of passionate intensity.

Before arriving in Canada in 1923, Frederic Lord was one of Britain's most respected conductors, composers and teachers. In Canada he became known as a composer of choral, orchestral and piano works. While he was in Brantford he taught music, composed, and organized the Canadian Choir which enjoyed enormous success on its tours to New York (Carnegie Hall), Albert Hall in London and throughout Canada. What he brought to Sheila's attention was his own solid tradition of craftsmanship and structure, an understanding of orchestral coloration and balance, and the sweeping virtuoso technical writing of his own keyboard works.

If we wonder today why such an eminent musical person would settle in Brantford it was because, at that time, Brantford was one of Ontario's top musical communities. This was still in the era when a network of musical-educational-concert centres existed throughout the Commonwealth, in the smaller centres as well as in the larger cities, where top people from London (and, on a lesser scale, Sydney and Montreal) would settle for various periods of time in order to teach, conduct church choirs and orchestral ensembles, and otherwise develop the local musical life with the purpose of touring what they had developed. Such a system produced an interest in, and set a very high performance standard of, classical music among the general population throughout Canada, Australia and New Zealand throughout the '30s, '40s and

'50s, and especially in the main population centres such as southern Ontario. Most of the Canadian Choir members were Brantford-born-and-raised; without the influence of this system many might never have had the opportunity to expand their musical knowledge and skills. Today the Canadian nationalist sympathies discourage this kind of learning exchange, perhaps to the country's detriment, it is too soon to tell. But it does restrict the kind of learning experience Sheila was able to get at that time. With her natural curiosity for all music, Sheila absorbed this new input with her customary dedication and fervour. Once again, she was in good hands.

Within weeks of Sheila's arrival in Brantford she was making musical headlines. She was ten-and-a-half years old, enrolled in school, and within a very short time was giving recitals and doing charity appearances in the city. Frederic Lord thought very highly of Sheila, so much so that he arranged for an interview with the Brantford *Expositor's* music critic, J.M. Merriman. Merriman took the usual tack, which every interviewer would in the future, outlining her as a child prodigy musically and intellectually, mentioned her "Shirley Temple" years and predicted that before very long she would "blossom forth as one of the 'musical finds' of the day". Since the interview took place after a concert, he also did his job as a music critic — Sheila's first "serious" press review.

> The young artist sang a number of songs and then played a couple of numbers with commendable aplomb. Her voice is remarkably mature for one of such tender years, the tones are well rounded, bright and clear, and her diction is astonishingly good.
>
> At the piano she demonstrated much technical ability and played with assurance and skill. Although Sheila possesses an abundance of confidence, she is a natural, unaffected youngster whose announced ambition is to become a concert pianist and grand opera singer. Frequent appearances in public during the past several years have given her much assurance but, nevertheless, have not in any visible way resulted in making her abnormally cognizant of her unusual talents and ability to put them to practical use.

Frederic Lord was quoted in the same article as saying that "Sheila shows unusually great promise as a concert pianist and I feel confident that, if she keeps her head, she will go a long way up the ladder to musical fame. In regard to her vocal ability, Sheila shows great natural aptitude for singing. Her voice is remarkably mature. She positively is one in a thousand. . . ."

In the overview, her stay would not be notable at all except for the influence of Lord. To this point, her cultural emphasis — both musically and in terms of psychological influence — had been upon the intensely involved spiritual and intellectual-humanistic questioning of the social issue conscious Winnipeg Jewish community. Brantford was her first introduction to the "East", as it is known in Western Canada, and Lord stressed the English influence, musically: establishmentarian-Royal-Anglican outlook with its atten-

Mr. and Mrs. Frederic Lord, Sheila, age 10, in the middle. (Brantford, Ontario)

dant musical values of courtly grace, a certain sense of semi-detachment defined by minute attention given to meticulous phrasing, light, airy lilting melodies and the rationalistic as opposed to emotional, religious devotion. They are two major influences which, even though mutually friendly when they come into contact, emphasized different aspects of music and different sensibilities. Because she was such an extraordinarily fast learner and absorber, and could literally, particularly musically, "put" herself into any frame of mind, it characterized for Sheila a total fusion of the emotional and rational rather than the merely rational. It was this natural fusion, which is so rarely achieved, which was from that time on to mark Sheila as eventually being one of the world's great pianists of her generation. The fact that she was exposed to these apparent dichotomies at a very young age when she was maleable and easily influenced was of great benefit to her as a pianist. The effect it had on her psychologically — that is, the Sheila who was not the musician (and at this age it seems apparent that almost all of her was "musician") is impossible to tell. Although she was in the local school only a brief time, she seemed to have made friends much more quickly and easily than she had in Winnipeg, for when she returned to Brantford two years later for a scheduled concert, the hall was filled with cheering schoolmates. As Mr. Merriman's review suggests, there was a naturalness in Sheila which, within the perhaps more understanding and sophisticated centres of Ontario, was appreciated in spite of her prodigy — 'freak of nature' — status in achievements.

PART II
The Promising Newcomer

Sheila Henig, age 17

The Promising Newcomer

At the time the Henigs arrived in Toronto World War II was nearing the end. Hitler was defeated and within a few months Hiroshima would signify the fall of the Japanese. A new era of optimism and faith in a better, more prosperous, peaceful, future rooted in technological progress dawned; an era which would last for nearly a quarter of a century before the realization that 'technological progress' had side effects and prosperity turned into unmanagable inflation. In the mid-'40s, however, the mood was, on the whole, one of genuine revolutionary change for the better. India's independence ushered in the end of European colonialism, and the State of Israel was born, despite the flip-flop efforts of the British labour government to squelch it.

A new spirit of buoyancy and prosperity swept through North America right after the war, a spirit of the good life which had not existed since the fateful October of 1929. The feeling of growth and new prosperity was especially keen in Toronto, which was just beginning to be transformed by the rush of progress from a provincial capital of 650,000 in 1945 to the major cosmopolitan metropolis of over two million people which it is today.

Unlike many American cities, time and progress have been good to Toronto. A formerly grubby downtown whose only claim to fame was that it contained (and still does contain) the second largest concentration of banks and financial institutions after New York, was beginning to become classy and modern. The formerly doughty main east-west artery of Bloor Street would eventually be transformed into one of North America's three most fashionable shopping thoroughfares (along with New York's Fifth Avenue and Beverly Hills' Rodeo Drive). Yorkville, which was then just a residential back-street two blocks north of Bloor, would become notorious — in a city least known for notoriety — during the hippy years and would change face several times before it settled into a chic off-Bloor Street shopping/eating area. Ancient dingy Victorian municipal structures, which had seen far better days, were being abandoned for North America's most boldly designed city hall. The city and its suburbs would soon be amalgamated into Metro Toronto which to this day remains North America's original ideal model of successful city-and-environ administration.

The city's predominantly Anglo-Saxon population makeup would forever become a thing of the past, making way for waves of postwar immigrants from Italy, Eastern Europe, and Portugal; then from the West Indies, Hong Kong, India and Pakistan. Toronto would become the fourth largest Italian city in the world. A city of white, English-background majority would become a city of minorities, forcing it to bypass the simplistic majority-rules system and devise a workable method of dealing with the urban polyglot and its troublesome offshoots. If in 1945 it was primarily a "roast-beef" city, in 1980 it would be known for its vast array of intriguing restaurants and epicurian delights of all nationalities.

Older established ethnic groups rapidly changed locale and lifestyle during this time. After decades of residence in and around the colourful open-air Kensington Market in the downtown core, Toronto's 90,000 Jews, buoyed by a new postwar prosperity, moved almost en masse further north, leaving the wide tenement-lined lower Spadina Avenue behind for the parklike suburban atmosphere of Forest Hill, and their offspring would furnish the city's growing artistic community with achievement-oriented youngsters, particularly in the music field. The arts generally would have to wait another two decades before the rough-neck outspoken theatre and art people would come into their own and be the backbone of "Canada first" nationalism. The city which sported only one major theatre (devoted to imports) in 1945, plus one or two indigenous theatres which invariably died from lack of support, boasted at its peak (in the 70s) twenty-seven live-play theatres, most of which were indigenous.

The Henigs hold on prosperity was very tenuous indeed for their first couple of years in the city. Harry Henig, in time, would be known as the "King of Spadina" and a leader in the ladies wear retail trade, but he started out as a partner in a clothing store on Queen Street. His partner, who later became a silent partner in their joint business, wanted someone who didn't necessarily have experience or money, but who was willing to work hard. Their first home was a small mice-infested flat on Palmerston Avenue near Dundas Street; their upstairs neighbours were two prostitutes who made the best of the dwindling soldier trade in '45, but it was good enough business at the time that the Henigs were aware of clomping boots on the stairs at fairly frequent intervals. Sheila, age eleven, spent her Saturdays in her father's store hemming dresses for the customers. It did not seem an ideal beginning but by the time two years were completed, Harry Henig had managed to move his family into a nice neighbourhood in Forest Hill.

Just as she had in Winnipeg and Brantford, Sheila was making a name for herself in Toronto music circles. She had barely enrolled in the Conservatory and she was giving recitals; she was winning awards for the first time in her life; she was competing regularly in the Kiwanis Music Festival and came out with first class honours in both singing and piano. By the time she was 15, she was presented with her fifth prize, this one for singing.

When she was 13 she returned to Brantford in the role of "assisting artist" in the second concert presented by the Brantford Collegiate Institute and Vocational School Glee Club. Two months later the Toronto Star announced she was one of four music students awarded the Diamond Jubilee Scholarship (piano) by the Royal Conservatory. Sheila's supreme effort was beginning to pay off. The Brantford concert had particular appeal for her because she "felt I was among friends". There is no need to elaborate on the reception of her performance, for the Brantford *Expositor* was effusive on the subject. " . . . Judging from the applause she received after each selection, whether it was vocal or piano, she definitely was among friends — some of whom were youngsters with whom she had attended Major Ballachey School, some of whom were people who had known her when she had studied music in Brantford a couple of years ago, and some of whom had become her friends as they listened to her sing and play." For the first time in a review the music selection received attention and an evaluation of her technique was attempted, a sure sign that she was being taken seriously. "Sheila Henig contributed four groups to the program, two each of vocal and piano selections.

"Her first group was composed of three Chopin compositions, Ecossaises, "Prelude in E Minor", and "Fantasy Impromptu". Here her versatility on the piano was apparent as she moved from the lilting Ecossaises to the deep-moving Prelude in E Minor.

"Her absorption in her playing was complete, and she proved her youthful memory to be highly retentive by playing all her selections without scores. Refreshing to her audience was her simple, almost shy manner of receiving their applause, and her unaffected conduct on the stage."

The review continued, listing the other piano selections — "Arabesque (No. 1 in E Major) (Debussy); "The Lark" (Glinka) and "The Hungarian" (MacDowell), with "The Hunting Song" (Mendelssohn) as an encore. The vocal selections included songs by Handel, Bury, Mallison, Cox, Greig and Sibella.

Sheila was also enrolled as a regular high school student at Forest Hill Collegiate, and she seemed to enjoy considerable personal popularity amongst her schoolmates, although her social life, as always, was almost non-existent. Piano was taking the edge over singing, but she had yet to make a firm decision on the matter and would, in fact, always maintain her singing techniques even while she was in the midst of the most rigorous piano training. It was around this time that her father bought her her first baby grand piano — $5,000 which had to be paid off on time — and her reaction to it was, as with everything that crossed her path, larger than life. "She couldn't get over it, she slept with that piano for weeks," her father remarked. "She was so proud of it — 'What a piano', she would say — 'It just sings, it just vibrates under my fingers' . . ." And Harry Henig remembers it did just that, it wasn't just playing. "She could extract something out of that piano that you would think wasn't there. She was actually living it, she and music and the piano, you couldn't separate them."

It is this kind of intense emotional response which is essential for the great performer, whether they be actor, musician, singer, dancer. It is the same energy needed to create the 'great love affair' and it is not surprising that Sheila stood on the sidelines while her peers were exploring their first crushes, their first puppy loves and generally throwing themselves into the 'dating game'. It was not that she did not understand this aspect of human development, for there was always a half-acknowledged longing for a normal social life and a somewhat dimmed realization that there was a whole element of her teenage development which she would one day have to account for and maybe have to pay the piper a higher price than she wanted to. She had all the surface qualities of a charmer — and she was indeed a genuinely charming and thoughtful human being — but the ambition of the performer would always win out.

During her high school years, Sheila's pianistic development progressed smoothly at the Conservatory. Canada's nationalists today debunk this period — roughly 1945-53 — as the heyday of Canada's "colonial mentality". It is seen as a time when Canada's culture was an artificial, academic hand-me-down imposition from London which had no true indigenous roots in authentic Canadian existence, which is very true. The most respected resident composer at the time was Healey Willan (of whom more will be said later) whose chief inspiration was English late-romantic rather than indigenous-Canadian or the then contemporary moderns such as Bartok, Hindemith and Prokofieff. From an interpretive and instructional standpoint, however, the musical preferences of the Royal Conservatory, which did encourage a genuine interest in classical musical excellence, were extremely positive. Serious music of a high quality was, at the time, appreciated amongst grass-roots Canadians, more so than their American counterparts where serious music was confined largely to a few large urban centres. Media criticism, what there was of it, was much more serious-music oriented than it is now. And this serious music atmosphere, aside from its particular adherent to London emulative models, did encourage a world outlook on culture and a sense of wordly sophistication. What this particular atmosphere did foster, however, and this may very well be at the root of the claims put forth by the nationalists, was a tendency to develop a cultural inferiority complex in Canada as opposed to England, or more recently, America. The story of Sheila Henig is not meant to serve as a thin disguise for an argument pro or con Canadian cultural nationalism, although she herself was to be one of the major victims of this peculiar Canadian outlook. It suffices to say that during those formative study years when potential greatness is being formed and tested, the instruction Sheila received from the Royal Conservatory of Music in Toronto, from Margaret Miller Brown and her other teachers, was as technically good and sufficiently world-outlook-oriented as she could have received almost anywhere at the time.

Sheila made time for other, lighter musical pursuits. She turned in an extremely professional performance as the Captain's daughter Josephine in the Forest Hill Collegiate's presentation of Gilbert & Sullivan's satirical operetta, *H.M.S. Pinafore.* The production itself was unusually professional for its amateur status and boasted a cast of 92. The local reviewer described Sheila as being "wistful, sweet and as pretty a captain's daughter to make any sailor, or anyone else, defy a pompous old fool like Sir Joseph to win her hand. But let's not let our feelings become too strong."

"Josephine's acting and voice were excellent indeed."

This was her second G&S performance with the school. The year previous to this she had appeared in *Pirates of Penzance* while at the same time preparing for her Conservatory exams. She worked herself to complete exhaustion, was bedridden right up to the day of the performance and it was only sheer will

Sheila, performing in *HMS Pinafore* at Forest Hill Collegiate.

power that got her on stage to, as usual, excellent reviews. One can't help but wonder why she would take on this kind of responsibility a second time.

Among her fellow-performers, and schoolmates for that matter, was Srul Irving Glick, son of a Toronto cantor, who was enormously impressed with her work. He would eventually go on not only to compose music for her but also to produce concerts and records for her in his capacity as a serious music producer at the CBC.

Amidst all this flurry of activity, Sheila hadn't forgotten her old friends. She was still corresponding with Carol, albeit sporadic and haphazard as ever. This particular letter sums up pretty well the telling strain on Sheila as her high school years came to an end.

July 26, 1951
Dear Carol:
You are probably thinking I have forgotten you. I assure you that this is not the case. Many added responsibilities have come into my life. Some are of a daily routine. Others are entirely unexpected, as you'll see when you read the enclosed newspaper clippings. As you know, I have become deeply involved in music since we moved to Toronto. The recitals at the Conservatory, singing lessons, piano lessons, and of course, piano and voice exams. All of this is terribly important to me, although it made my head spin for a while. Thank God it's all behind me now. I passed with first-class honours in both. I have also been awarded another scholarship by the Royal Conservatory of Music.

I am now seeking an island of peace where I can take a respite, re-evaluate my work, my ambitions, and come to terms with myself. I think that I'm really too young to cope with so many responsibilities. They weigh too heavily on my mind. Perhaps I should withdraw from it all for at least one year, before I enter the University of Toronto, which would allow me some time to make up my mind what I really want to do with my life. I often think that I would like to major in languages or journalism. They were my best subjects. I got nine firsts out of eleven. When I do reach a decision on this matter, I may be in a position to extricate myself somewhat from the stage and cut down on concerts.

[later] It seems as though it wasn't meant to be. I have just received a letter from the University of Toronto in which I'm informed that I have been awarded a three-year free-tuition scholarship in the Faculty of Music. I am very happy with the award, of course, but it somehow changed all of my plans. I'm sometimes frightened when I recount my good fortune which has continued for some years; but I am thankful for thus having the

opportunity to pursue my musical career, and I can't help wondering where all of this will lead me to. At the moment, I dare not think of the consequences.

Your friend,
Sheila

Carol didn't answer her until the following December, and then it was to relay the information that her mother had died. "She'd never complained of being ill, but I have lately noticed that she didn't look her usual self. As you know, we live on a farm where one hardly ever thinks of going to a doctor in Calgary unless one is seriously ill. One morning, when she didn't show up in the kitchen as usual, Scot and I went looking for her, and found her in our small den. She was dead.

My life now seems unreal and insecure. My father walks around in silence as if he was in a stupor. Scot, although he is older than I, is searching my face for some strength and consolation, but I don't have any to give him. He clings quietly to his grief and sheds tears when no one sees. Oh, Scot, if only I could help you; but I am so helpless myself.

One evening the three of us finally had a heart-to-heart talk, and expressed our grief openly to each other. My father hinted that he might sell the farm and move to Vancouver. Should that happen I would be the saddest person in the world. It's your letters, my friend, which are vibrant and full of enthusiasm, that make my life somewhat bearable.

Your friend,
Carol.

Sheila expressed her sorrow for her friend as best she could, in her own way — *Life, my dear Carol, is like the seasons of the year. The bleak autumn comes after sunny summer days, and the cold winter is sure to follow. I can't tell you not to grieve, but you know that what's destroyed cannot be mended, and what's passed can't be recaptured. This especially applies to mothers. Everyone loves a mother, although there are times when we don't show our love. However, mourning as was understood by Freud serves a profound need in human beings. It provides time during which we can become adjusted emotionally to the loss we have sustained, so that we can heal again. I'm feeling so very helpless that I can't put into words how sorry I am. We are all living with hopes and aspirations. It's therefore essential that we understand how to accept life in its proper perspective and you, my friend, are no exception. We are somehow compelled to live the kind of life destiny had chosen for us.*

Take me as an example, Sheila continued. "It would be ungrateful on my part to feel that I have been cheated out of being a child. Even though I know that such thoughts will come to me countless times in the future, I nevertheless ask myself constantly: 'Does the sacrifice justify the cause'. I *can't come up with an honest answer. I have been exposed to, and gradually saturated with, music ever since I can remember. Would it be fair, even if it were possible, to make a complete change in my life? My mind says yes, but my heart and soul reject it.*

"*... From the description you have given me about your farm, I visualize it and your father and brother. I have also formed a mental image of your house, the barn, and all the animals living there in tranquility. The hypnotic horizon at twilight and the deafening sweet stillness at dawn. The refreshing evening breeze that's soothing to your face in the cool of the night. The glistening dew on the green grass when the sun begins to rise while you are sound asleep.*

Time seems to be my worst enemy. I have much to do but not enough time to do it in. It seems that each individual is destined to a certain kind of life so let's be thankful and have faith in tomorrow. Take heart, my friend. Be strong and try to adjust to the present which seems unbearable to you at this point in time.

Sheila's spirits picked up and she continued on with renewed energy. *And now it's my turn. I'm going out with a boy who has taken a liking to me. His name is Bill. He takes me to a movie occasionally or we just sit around and chat. I, too, am sort of fond of him. He seems very nice; his name has a homey, good-natured reassuring ring to it. Although I can't spare the time to go out with him as often as he would like me to, I do enjoy his company whenever I have the time. I'm also attracted to him and like to be with him. What I resent most is that he dropped out of school, which I find difficult to accept.*

I am aware of the fact that my parents don't like to see me going out, since they claim that I'm too young, but I can't see anything wrong with it. I'm not marrying the boy; I just want to have someone to talk to when I can afford the time. The years fly by so quickly that I never have enough hours in a day. It frightens me sometimes.

Will write again soon.

> *Your friend,*
> *Sheila*

It was quite true, Sheila's parents didn't like the idea of boyfriends. Bill was a boxer and quit high school for a while. They sent her to a music camp for the summer as a counsellor hoping it would discourage any further association. They hadn't reckoned on Bill's determination.

Camp Kiwagama was deep in the Haliburton bush and inaccessible from the mainland except by taking a boat from Dorset to the island. Although he didn't have a car, Bill found a way of getting to Sheila.

He started out on a Saturday morning hitch-hiking to Dorset and didn't have too much difficulty in getting rides up to the point where the road branches out into many miles of thick hilly forest. He decided to walk the rest of the way: cars hardly ever passed through this desolate stretch of country. Darkness and rain closed in on him as he slowly struggled along the trail. About ten hours after he left Toronto he finally reached Dorset, soaking wet, bruised and completely exhausted. He managed to rent a small boat from the harbour watchman and got across to see Sheila. When he returned to Toronto after the weekend, he recounted his ordeal to Sheila's parents, letting them know, not very subtlely, that he was a determined young man indeed.

When Sheila returned from summer camp they took up where they'd left off. Her parents were terribly upset, they felt that she was too young and belonged to a different world than Bill's. Sheila had had a hard childhood in more ways than she probably recognized; she was a child of the depression, as well as being a prodigy; she had known hunger as well as glittering attention. Briefly, her father thoughtfully summed it up: "Sheila's formative years were very difficult. She was burning up with ambition, she was obsessed with an incredible urge to make it big one day in the music world. Every day of her young life was filled with excitement and also frustration, trying to achieve her goal. Every day presented a new challenge to her restless soul."

For the next two summers Sheila studied at the Chatauqua Music Camp with the eminent teacher, James Friskin, of the Juilliard School of Music, and appeared as soloist several times with the Chatauqua Symphony Orchestra. However, this didn't discourage Bill from visiting her every other weekend. There was just no way her parents could stop him from seeing her. The two young people seemed to be star-crossed, for in all logic, they were unsuited for each other. Sheila was intensely ambitious, while Bill was a slow-moving, easy-going type; two extremes on a collision course, so her parents thought. Fanny Henig cautioned Sheila many times — "You can't make him happy, you're dedicated to your music and he just doesn't have the kind of ambition that you have." Sheila insisted they were just friends, her mother and father were taking it too seriously. And as far as Sheila was concerned, at that time, this is the way it was; the only thing she was projecting into the future was her music career.

Somehow the relationship didn't snuff itself out during Sheila's university years, for the pressure, which she applied to herself, of having to live up to the honour of winning three years free tuition was almost unbearable and to her parents knowledge, nobody else, not even themselves, could get near her. Harry Henig recalls it as the worst years they had had to put in with Sheila. When she was in the house, she was practicing; nobody could breathe, they couldn't even turn a tap on to get a drink of water because any sound whatsoever disturbed her concentration. Once again, doors and windows were tightly shut; the family moved to the basement from 4 p.m. to 11 p.m. Louise, in grade school at the time and learning to play the flute, had to practice in their garage for Sheila couldn't bear the sound of the 'beginner'. After eleven o'clock, Sheila would stop practising and the family could come upstairs, Mrs. Henig could wash the dishes and the rest of them could go about getting ready for bed. Weekends were worse for Sheila was home all day. For three years she completely isolated herself from her family and entered another world. She communicated very little with her parents during this period; after seven hours of practising she was too tired to talk, she fell into bed and started the whole cycle again the next day. It seemed unfair — " . . . and it was unfair," Mr. Henig remarked. "But what can you do when you're blessed with a brilliant child with a ferocious drive." Although Sheila's dedication was intense enough during her Conservatory and high school years, she would take the time to sit on the porch on a summer night with her father and chat with him.

For a long time Sheila had levelled almost equal determination towards a singing career as towards the piano. In the Kiwanis Festival she had performed in both categories and had won several first class awards in operatic solos, her last (the fifth) being 1952 for the coloratura soprano (very high pitch) in a foreign language. The time had arrived, however, when she had to decide which she was going to pursue, piano or voice. Although she did have a beautifully expressive high soprano voice, Sheila felt that it was just not good enough for opera and she therefore chose to major in piano. She gave her first complete solo piano recital at the Royal Conservatory Concert Hall in the late afternoon on January 20, 1953.

The pieces she chose to perform spanned the period of 1800-1950, the period of music which permitted total emotional involvement to its maximum. Sheila, being an emotionally intense person, naturally felt most comfortable performing music which originated between the baroque (Bach) and the formal classicism of Mozart and Haydn, and the scientistic period exemplified by John Cage and Karlheinz Stockhausen — beginning with Beethoven (who concluded the formal classical style of Mozart and Haydn and invented the freer romantic style later utilized by Schubert and Chopin), proceeding through Chopin and Lizst, into the mild but extremely stimulating and inventive dissonance of Debussy, Ravel and the other music impressionists, and concluding with the free-form dissonant, melodic abstractionist masters such as Prokofieff, Hindemith and Bartok.

One of Sheila's greatest musical virtues was her interest in performing lesser-known compositions which were musically unique. She took great pleasure in 'discovering' an obscure composition, practising and perfecting it with very few emulative models on record or tape, then presenting it to an unfamiliar audience and finally, positively winning that audience with that piece of music. As her professional career matured she would attempt to do this at every concert she performed. It is probably this attribute which prompted many of her colleagues to declare her a genuine connoisseur of music.

She knew her own emotional inclinations best and this is why she rarely performed pure, unarranged Bach, which requires a greater degree of emotional detachment she was musically honest enough to admit was not part of her personality. It is also the reason why she never explored the dissonant scientistic and emotionally-dry avant garde composers which characterized some of the serious music of the post-1950 period.

Thus, in her Royal Conservatory solo debut, Sheila opened with Beethoven's piano *Sonata opus 53,* not one of Beethoven's overly familiar "showpiece" sonatas of the grand-stroke bravura style such as the *Pathetique* or the *Moonlight* or the *Appassionata,* all of which were written later. Neither was it one of his very early sonatas which still resembled the formal courtly classical style of Mozart of Haydn. Following the intermission, Sheila performed the four-movement *Sonata #3* by the contemporary American composer Norman Dello Joio who, along with Aaron Copland, incorporated American jazz and pop styles into a late-romantic European framework (Dello Joio tended to be a bit more abstract than Copland). She then went on to perform the whimsically impressionistic *Feux Follets* by the Quebec composer Phillipp, followed by the Debussy impressionist works, *Les Sons et Les Parfums* and *Tourent dans l'air du Soir.* She concluded with Chopin's *Ballade in G minor.* Frederic Chopin, the crown jewel of the romantic era, wrote four Ballades which are considered to be his most intricately develped solo piano works, far beyond the scope of his more popular (then) waltzes, mazurkas and polonaises.

Winters in Toronto are grey, damp and dismal, but they rarely approach the harsh bitter cold regularly occurring every year in Winnipeg. Summers, on the other hand, can be much more uncomfortable. One of the outstanding examples of just how uncomfortable a Toronto summer can be came in late August and early September of that same year — 1953 — when for twelve straight days, the temperature climbed over the 90-degree (fahrenheit) mark and for the first four days of September, it reached 100 degrees and over. Toronto would witness intense heat waves before and after, but for sheer length the torrid spell would never be equalled. What made this scorcher even more miserable was the fact that since it occurred so late in the summer, families had already returned home from summer vacations and the kids were all home from summer camps. So the vast majority of Torontonians were sweltering it out in the city. And, a great many of them were at the Canadian National Exhibition, which is held at the end of the summer instead of during its height precisely because the weather is usually more pleasant then.

A Toronto tradition, the C.N.E. is the largest outdoor annual fair of any kind held anywhere in the world. For those who have not been lucky enough to have ever attended it, it is a two-week long potpourri of agricultural fairs, trade fairs, giant noisy amusement park, bazaar and dance hall held every summer from approximately the middle of August through the labour day weekend, in a series of permanent rococo-Victorian arenas on the Lake Ontario waterfront about two miles west of downtown Toronto. The circus atmosphere of the exhibition is such archetypal kitsch and tacky gaudiness that it retains a distinctive high-camp style all its own that can't be matched anywhere else. The annual fair also signals the greatest concentration of "competitions" — of all kinds, shapes and sizes — of the year. In 1953 the annual CNE Star Free Concert $500 senior piano scholarship competition was held on the fair grounds. Sheila and six other finalists battled for five days during that torrid August-September in an auditorium which was not air-conditioned.

Such conditions were probably the most gruelling that Sheila — or, for that matter, any pianist — would ever have to face. She won the competition in what must have been a supreme test of strength and endurance for atop the usual rigours of competitive nervousness was the necessity of exhibiting flawless technique and a high degree of emotional sensitivity usually not encouraged by a temperature of 110 degrees and a humidity of at least ninety per cent. The judges were Cyril Hampshire of Hamilton, Ontario, a popular adjudicator and music teacher, and composer-conductor Alexander Brott, who founded and conducted the McGill Chamber Orchestra of Montreal and whose two sons, Dennis and Boris, are today high-profile achievers in Canadian music.

Reading the decision of both judges, Cyril Hampshire said that Sheila Henig's performance of Felix Mendelssohn's sparklingly delicate but technically intricate *Rondo Capriccioso* ". . . left absolutely no doubt as to who was winner. In her interpretation, she made something of everything". The Star's reporter made a particular note of the "boiling weather".

This CNE prize was Sheila's "baptism by fire" into the world of musical competitions. From then on her academic, and eventually, professional music career was to progress by leaps and bounds. In the midst of this chaotic time in her life when she was in university and preparing for concerts and competitions, she was demanding a response from Carol to her letters — futile, as it turned out, for Carol didn't reply until the following summer.

July 27, 1954
Dear Carol,
This is the fifth letter I've written you since I last heard from you over a year ago. I am terribly worried that something happened to you to prevent you from writing. I have a lot of good news that I'm bursting to tell you, but I am waiting to hear from you.
Your friend,
Sheila

Sheila's next big milestone was being named winner of the $1,000 scholarship awarded by the Timothy Eaton Company, Canada's oldest department store chain, granted to the student graduating with the highest standing from the Faculty of Music at the University of Toronto. In 1955, Sheila twice performed as guest pianist with the Toronto Symphony Orchestra which was then in its last season under the twenty-five year reign of Sir Ernest MacMillan. She was also featured in concerts over CBC Radio and the newly-formed CBC television network.

The Eaton scholarship was the latest of a total of eight awards which had been given to Sheila. Besides the CNE senior piano scholarship, she had won six scholarships at the Royal Conservatory. She had been able to acquire one of the best fundamental musical educations available anywhere in the world virtually tuition-free. Now she planned to branch out beyond Toronto and use the Eaton scholarship to continue her studies in New York with that city's most famous and venerable piano teacher, Rosinna Lhevine. Probably the best-known pupil of Miss Lhevine's is Van Cliburn, the tall Texan who three years later won the Moscow International Tchaikovsky Competition, performing Tchaikovsky's *Piano Concerto in B-flat*. He and Sheila were both the same age; both were highly regarded by Miss Lhevine. Sheila's impressive cache of awards placed her in good standing wherever serious music circles existed. Her contacts in New York soon recommended that she enter the intense competition for the coveted Naumburg award to be granted in the spring of 1956. She immediately set to work.

June 12, 1955, Sheila finally received a reply from Carol, and this began, for these two anyway, a brief flurry of exchanges. After a bit of chit-chat, Carol gave Sheila some happy news.

June 12, 1955
Dear Sheila,

Peter and I intend to get married just as soon as father sells the farm at which time he and Scot will move to Vancouver. The thought of being left alone in Calgary is quite unpleasant. I'll miss my only two, who are so very dear to my heart. I hope that Peter will be good to me. He promised me he would be. I, on the other hand, will have to let go of the past and start for myself a new life and hopefully a good future.

I have to go now. Peter is waiting in his car for me.

Love,
Carol

July 26, 1955
Dear Carol,

I received your letter which made me extremely happy to learn that you're on the threshold of getting married. I congratulate you and wish you all the luck in the world. You certainly deserve it. Perhaps it's fate, or should I attribute it to coincidence?

I too, have good news to tell you. I'm deliriously happy to inform you that I won the Eaton award which automatically pays me $1,000. The second thing is: my boyfriend Bill proposed to me. He asked me to marry him while we were driving home from Detroit. Although I have been going out with him for a few years, and I have become rather fond of him, it nevertheless came as quite a shock to me. He is a nice easy-going boy, about my age, which is really unimportant. He is not familiar with classical music but he is willing to learn to appreciate it. The fact that he is an athlete makes *it the more interesting to me. I have always been fascinated by athletic types, especially by boxers and skaters. They possess so much stamina, courage and dedication to their profession; they should be admired. Boxing to my way of thinking is a cruel sport, but I nevertheless enjoy watching a good boxing match. Last week he took me to Detroit to watch him box his second professional bout. It was very exciting; perhaps too much so. I practically got hysterical during the bout. I was screaming and yelling at the top of my lungs, hitting people with a newspaper who sat in front of me. On the way home, I expressed my feelings about fighters quite clearly. I told him that it was emotionally exhausting for me to watch him enter the ring and clobber or be clobbered to submission and unconsciousness. Needless to say, my throat was sore for a week after that fight.*

The remainder of the letter took on an unusual cast for Sheila, for it was as if she was talking to herself rather than Carol. She had many times unburdened herself to her friend with a degree of self-expression she couldn't seem to achieve in a verbal exchange, but this was the most deeply introspective moment of their correspondence.

While Bill was driving the car, I curled up in a corner and tried to think things out. What does music really mean to me and how will it affect my life if I marry Bill? When I am performing, I am actually reaching out to humanity. I am trying to bring enjoyment to those who appreciate classical music, and perhaps also reach those who have no feelings for my type of music. I am forever hoping that through my playing I'll open hearts and doors that are tightly shut, and create a third or even a fourth dimension. If I will be successful, even to a small degree, this would be my reward. One thought, however, kept nagging at me. How can I possibly love someone who is living in a different world, dreams different dreams, and whose ambitions are entirely different from mine?

I have chosen my destiny. I made my mind up to be a performer, and wish to dedicate my life to music. Or am I perhaps expecting too much of myself? Will it really happen the way I think? I simply don't know. Should I, at the risk of my career, commit my future to someone who is the complete opposite to my world and my ambitions? Would it be possible for me to share my life with Bill who would perhaps agree to some sort of compromise without hindering my dreams and aspirations? The thought of having to share my life with him was not really my ambition and yet I found it irresistible despite the regrets that I might have years later.

All these thoughts came to me in a jumble, they weren't nearly as clear then as the way I say them now. I started talking to Bill and I did give him one ultimatum — he could either continue his boxing career and forget that we ever met or go back to school. He was willing to agree. We talked on and on about what he might take and the conclusion of it all is that by the time we

reached Toronto, he had decided on Pharmacy. That night he gave me his
solemn promise that he would continue with his education. In spite of my
doubts and apprehension our destiny was sealed and I realized that I really
did love him.

> *My mother worries about me. She keeps on telling me that I am*
> *expecting too much of myself; that I'm constantly reaching for a*
> *perfection that no one else has ever achieved. "Even a perfectionist*
> *can never be perfect," she says, "and you are not about to be the first*
> *one to reach that unreachable summit". I often wonder if it's worth*
> *the effort and I come up with the same answer: Yes, to me, it's worth*
> *it. I am happiest when I perform. I pour my heart and soul out when*
> *I play. I feel a joy and happiness and sorrow which I try to express*
> *in my performance. This is my life in its entirety and I love it.*
> *Forgive me for digressing. I'll try not to do it again.*

Love
Sheila

Mr. Henig said that once the two of them had made the decision, he accepted it. Fanny Henig, however, tried once more to persuade her daughter to reconsider. Her concern was as much for Bill as for Sheila. More than anything else she prayed for her daughter's happiness, but in a marriage that was not enough. "Sheila, can you make him happy, too!" she cautioned her again.

William Sidney and Sheila Henig were married a little less than a month later, on August 21st, at Beth Sholom Synagogue in Toronto, and her parents saw to it that it was a grand wedding. They decided to live with Sheila's parents until Bill would graduate.

Mr. Henig remembers those five gruelling "pharmacy years" in an emotional way — Sheila's formal schooling was over and Bill's had just begun. "They were difficult for everyone, especially for Sheila," he remarked. "Sheila and Bill lived with us, and she had more than her career to worry about, she was determined to see Bill graduate some day. She was up nights helping him with his homework with the same enthusiastic intensity as she put into her own work, practicing the piano. And after those long, frustrating years Bill finally graduated. Sheila was deliriously happy that her perseverance had paid off."

Perhaps it was because her own university years were completed that she was able to devote this kind of energy to Bill — or, as she was to prove again and again throughout her life, the commitment to helping others seemed to add to her energy rather than deplete it. All told, it had been a gruelling decade for her since she arrived in Brantford. "They were difficult years," she remarked in the press once. "I was trying to live up to my professor's expectations and, of course, to the media." But this was behind her for, except for the occasional lesson in New York, Sheila was now launched on a professional career — and she was a young married woman, which would give her a status of social maturity and security, something she had never experienced before.

Sheila and husband, William Sidney, at their marriage.

Less than a month after their wedding, Carol wrote Sheila again. She did not necessarily empathize with Sheila's dedicated ambition as a concert pianist, but she definitely understood her.

My dear friend Sheila,

Reading your recent letter was quite a surprise to me. I suddenly realized that we have grown up. We have traversed many years since we got to know each other and the time has come when we feel at liberty to put on paper our innermost feelings. Thank you for the wedding pictures. I received them today. They are absolutely beautiful, especially the one in which you posed in front of a mirror. I am glad to hear that Bill has gone back to school. I hope that you'll be happy and your aspirations will be fulfilled. I am sure that the years will bring you the kind of rewards you deserve.

You are a genius, a gifted artist; your talent seems to shine through in everything you write. You're a performer, blessed with creativity and sensitivity which you express through your music. I imagine that your life is difficult, but it's worth the sacrifice, I suppose. You have apparently committed yourself to the concert stage. You have no choice now but to pursue your career, and give up many other things life has to offer.

I agree with your philosophy when you say that the best way not to be considered a genius, or, even an ordinary artist, and live a happy normal life is to avoid education entirely, or get rid of any you have been given. However, it's not what a person knows that's important but what he does with it. And it's not just doing things but understanding that what you do brings excitement and pleasure to your life. In your case, it's a natural reaction to a strong dedication that makes you unique. You want to do things which you feel you must. You have grown up in a different world which is frustrating and demanding; enjoyable, but also nerve-wracking at the same time. Failure to live up to your high expectations would be humiliating, and you would consider it a failure to art itself.

"I can feel the intensity in your writing, and your complete dedication to the music around which your life seems to evolve. I wish you success in your upcoming concerts, and please do keep in touch and take care.

Love,
Carol

PART III
The Professional

Sheila Henig and TSO conductor, Walter Susskind.

The Professional

The Naumburg Award competition was Sheila's first experience in a major competition. Newly married, she practiced seven and a half hours a day for a solid month in preparation. The preliminaries, which weeded out the contestants (in the 1956 competition 80 pianists from around the world started out, from which the judges would pick four finalists), were known to send very promising pianists scurrying for other careers. Sheila survived to become one of the four finalists, losing out in the final competition to George Katz of New York. She was the only woman amongst the finalists and the only Canadian. In previous years soprano Lois Marshall and violonist Betty Jean Hagan had won the Naumburg Award. The loss of the award didn't seem to discourage her for she returned to Toronto full of enthusiasm, resolving to compete again the following year. Realizing that she was a novice in international competitions — and this was a coveted one indeed — she was delightfully surprised to have made the finals at all. She radiated exhilaration when she talked with a Toronto Telegram reporter (April 10, 1956).

> "The experience was wonderful, but nerve-wracking," she admitted. "I loved every minute of it, particularly when I realized I was probably the only Canadian in the competition."
>
> . . . .
>
> This was Sheila's first experience in major competition. The week of playing and preliminary studies would probably make a labourer flinch. She practiced seven and a half hours daily for the past month.

There were many reasons beyond the Naumburg experience. Her professional career was, in those early years (as it is with so many "promising" musicians) meteoric. She drew accolades whenever she performed and it looked as if she was about to repeat the "baby Sheila" triumphs of her Winnipeg days, only this time she was going all the way. She became a newsworthy personality and the press liked to cover her from a personal angle as well as a professional one. She was beginning to be known as the "glamorous" contingent of classical music performers locally, for it was often remarked amongst friends and admirers that she *always* "looked like she just stepped off the pages of Vogue". Again, the *Toronto Telegram* picked up on this:

> DRESS POSES A PROBLEM FOR PIANIST
> "When pianist Sheila Henig goes shopping for a new dress, she usually goes alone. The reason: If she goes with any of her friends, they are apt to come away with the impression that there's something a little wrong with Sheila mentally
> "I try on a dress, then I start shrugging my shoulders this way and that way till I notice looks of growing consternation."

Buying a dress for a concert is not just a matter of getting something that fits, or even something that looks attractive. It also has to be something the pianist can play in comfortably. Hence the necessity for shoulder shrugging.

April 10, 1956

The article went on to quote Sheila about a fellow professional who was inclined to treat what she wore for a concert "with a degree of unconcern. She wore a dress with a crinoline. But she made the fatal error of not trying the dress on sitting down. When she sat down at the piano for the concert, the crinoline made an almost impassable barrier between her and the keyboard."

Next, the interviewer detailed her routine before a performance, de rigueur for 'star' interviews.

A steak and potatoes about four hours before going on stage is regular fare for her on the day of a concert.

As for nerves, she gets them out of her system the week before. As the concert looms closer, her nervous tension tends to wear itself out.

Practice on the day of the concert is kept to two hours at the outside. She usually plays through the concert work using the music.

"If you practice from memory on the day of the concert and happen to forget a passage, you can give yourself a mental block. I like to practice through slowly, using the music."

Despite the flurry of interest in the press about Sheila, the rest of that year, her first as a married woman, was uneventful professionally. She helped Bill, encouraging him through his first-year studies, and worked a lot on her own, knowing that the future was bright and the present would take care of itself. It is a pattern of ebb and flow in the life of Canadian musicians; the media, the powers-that-be, whatever or whoever it is, recognizes a good thing and then drops it. Her personal excitement, apart from a very happy year with her husband, was a puppy dog she and Bill secreted into her father's house, hiding it in the basement for its first night in its new home. Sheila quickly named it "Lassie", for the female dog was "as beautiful, intelligent and playful" as the original. Harry Henig and his wife heard whimpering in the basement early the next morning and were at first very puzzled as to where the little creature came from. "It took us about two minutes to realize that the whole thing had the mark of Sheila's hand on it — she and Bill had obviously slipped it into the house in the middle of the night." Mrs. Henig wasn't that happy, she had a full house to contend with, after all, but Sheila determined she would have at least two dogs and probably some cats when she and Bill had a place of their own.

"She loved animals," her father remarked, simply. "She had to have them around her."

The new year, 1957, entered with two concerts with the TSO Secondary School concert series and then a week later, a bravura performance in

Charlottetown. Walter Susskind had just taken over as conductor of the Toronto Symphony and it was probably Sheila's performance in the TSO school concerts (conducted by assistant conductor, Paul Scherman) which first brought her to his attention. These student concerts have become a tradition with the Symphony and continue to this day. They are very well attended — at this particular concert there were 2,000, most of them high school students. If anything, they have become even more popular over the years since the Toronto high school curriculum has increasingly emphasized the serious study of music as part of the regular graduate arts and science program, including providing instruments for all students who wish to take the course of studies. The two concerts contained almost identical programs, bringing in her best notices to date with the Liszt *First Piano Concerto in E Flat Major.* George Kidd of the *Toronto Telegram* reviewed in January 1957:

STRENGTH, ROMANTICISM IN PIANIST'S WORK

. . . .

Paul Scherman conducted the orchestra, and the usually very well behaved audience of about 2,000 students listened attentively to everything that went on. Most of the program had already been heard earlier this week.

Miss Henig has been steadily making a name for herself in the field of music, and last night she produced some of her best work as she played the Liszt First Piano Concerto in E Flat Major.

From the outset one could admire the strength that she possessed and the romanticism that gradually crept into her playing. She brought forth a gentle singing charm to the lyrical sections and balance with the orchestra was usually good, although in the finale the soloist was not always heard.

Her reading of the concerto was a sensitive and mature one that had considerable feeling and a poetic freedom that was always engaging. The dramatic passages were produced with clarity. Miss Henig overcame any possible technical problems with the skill of a true artist. She is obviously a pianist with a bright future.

. . . .

Sheila was particularly pleased with the reception of the concert; it had special meaning for her that her audience were students, most of them only a few years younger than herself. "It proves that there are still people who appreciate classical music despite the fact that we are living in a 'Rock'n' Roll' age", she remarked to a fellow musician, later.

If she was happy with the TSO concerts, she must have been dancing on stars with her Charlottetown debut, although, as the review remarked, this one wasn't well attended. "The only disappointment was the size of the audience; so much was enjoyed by so few despite a very low admission price." (Charlottetown *Patriot,* January 30, 1957). Those who did attend were in for a rare treat, it seemed. The reviewer rhapsodized — "One of the finest concerts ever given here was Miss Sheila Henig's piano recital at Prince of Wales College on Monday evening. Miss Henig is a rising star in Canadian music and those who heard her could understand why from the moment her magnificent hands first touched the keyboard to the glorious climax of Liszt's *Hungarian Rhapsody No. 2* which brought to a close a rare and memorable performance.... the grand piano at the College has been touched by a master who, we predict, will in the next few months bring American and European audiences cheering to their feet in tribute to a great young Canadian." As it turned out, it was more than a few months, it took a couple of years, but no more than that. In its closing tribute, the *Patriot* took the opportunity to suggest something more positive than just lamenting the small audience.

> We predict, too, that there would be magnificent results from a community policy of filling the halls for concerts, plays, and the like to hear local and national entertainment at their best. Everyone would not only be more conscious of his community, but happier when, in this hectic age, he would permit his soul to be touched from time to time by the forces of music, literature, and the theatre which have moved men and nations in every generation.

Eventually this would come to pass through the auspices of provincial arts councils and the national Canada Council; grants would become available locally and nationally for individual study and the promotion of Canadian talent across the country.

Sheila was pleasantly surprised with the review. She had taken the whole thing very calmly, as far as she was concerned she came out on stage, walked over to the piano and just played. She had not felt particularly high or "up" for the performance, more like an everyday practicing session. "Maybe I should take that approach more often," she remarked to Bill.

The rest of the winter she spent preparing for the Naumburg competition to be held again in the Town Hall in New York. Again, she was one of four finalists, but missed the prize. But that day, April 2, 1957, was memorable anyway.

She literally lept off the piano bench in New York and began a wild dash for Brantford, for she was scheduled to play in that city at 8:15 p.m.

It was a story in itself. She finished at the Town Hall at 3 p.m. and started the 400-mile dash for Brantford. It began with a cab-ride to Idlewild (now Kennedy) airfield. The plane left 25 minutes late, thus arriving late at Malton (now Toronto International) airport. Mr. and Mrs. Henig and Bill were waiting with a car to take her to Brantford but before that last 70 miles could be tackled she had to clear customs.

At 7:15, only an hour before she was due on stage, they got away from Malton and hit the highway, wildly exceeding the speed limit. A patrolman caught up with them in no time and more precious time was used up in explaining the urgency. But the policeman wasn't accepting excuses that night and handed them a ticket, and further frustrated the Henigs by tailing them for some miles. Finally, at 8:45, after a hurried change into a turquoise tulle evening dress and a glance at the program to see what she was playing, Sheila took her place at the piano, composed and smiling.

> Even as she played 'God Save the Queen', there was something about the firm, confident full-toned sounds she produced that promised an unusually interesting evening. The impression was speedily confirmed in three sonatas by Scarlatti. Here, there was high technical competence, marked by clean crisp fingering, excellent pace and phrasing, musical insight and above all, a rare, controlled strength.
> . . .

(Brantford Expositor, Apr. 3, 1957)

The program included a Beethoven sonata, *Symphonic Etudes* of Schumann, Chopin's *F Minor Fantasie* and Ravel's *Sonatine.* She closed the program with the *Hungarian Rhapsody,* then gave an encore. By the time the review went to press, the reporter had heard of the series of misadventures of the day and made the most of them. However, it was obviously no lightweight program she had to face at the end of the day, and it was one hell of a tired Sheila who leaned on her husband's shoulder on the drive home. Sheila's only comment the next day, whispered because she had laryngitis, was "You are only as good as your last performance . . . ." Then she remained silent and let her vocal chords unwind.

The final couple of years of the '50s and the beginning of the '60s produced a bumper crop of performances for Sheila. She rounded out 1957 by appearing in the first of what were to become fairly regular recitals in New York at the Steinway Concert Hall on 57th Street near 6th Avenue. There are certain areas in New York where 'collectibles' congregate and 57th and 6th was at that time, the heart of the classical music personalities and entourages. She loved, as any becoming pianist would at the age of 23, to be part of the glamour and energy associated with the New York classical music centre; to have her own solo recital was analogous to making it for the first time on Broadway.

At the end of the '50s Walter Susskind stepped into her life and gave her a great professional boost. Susskind had become conductor of the TSO in 1957 and Toronto musicians were feeling the excitement of his vitality. He replaced Sir Ernest MacMillan who had for 25 years nourished the orchestra to the position of solid reputation; if there was a lack anywhere it was in the orchestra's image: musically excellent but perhaps a little shy of chutzpah. Susskind would inject a large dose of this into the group and Seji Ozawa would shoot it to the top, making fine use of the musicians' collective expertise, adding a veneer of pizzazz usually reserved for the pop field.

Susskind's background was European — born in Prague in 1913 — and his career was notable because he used the 'guest conductor' route to great advantage. He began his career as assistant conductor of the Prague German Opera House at the age of 20; when the house closed in '38, he toured as recitalist and conductor for two years through 26 countries and finally settled in England, making it his home until the war was over. As soon as travel in Europe was possible, he was off again, guest conducting through Europe, Australia, South Africa and Israel until the Scottish National Orchestra contracted him as resident conductor. In 1953 he left Scotland for a three-year stint as conductor of the Victoria Symphony Orchestra in Melbourne, Australia, and then to Toronto. He considered the guest conducting role vital for his overall development, and he indeed became a versatile, cosmopolitan conductor. "Conductors learn from other conductors and they, in turn, learn from guest conductors. It seems we learn most from other orchestras, but we do our best work with our own." Susskind was a recital pianist in his own right, and although no conductor plays instrumental favourites, he was particularly fond of Sheila as a person and revered her as a pianist.

With almost messianic fervour, Susskind began to promote and elevate Toronto musicians and composers; his belief in them was unequivocal and he was singularly responsible for lifting the orchestra, en masse, into the ranks of the world's great orchestras. In the TSO's New York performance in 1963 he got a standing ovation not once, but twice: the first one for Lois Marshall and the orchestra performing Richard Strauss' *Four Last Songs,* and again with the performance of Dvorak's *Symphony No. 2.* The event prompted N.Y. *Herald-Tribune's* music critic, Eric Salzman, to comment: "It seems strange that Toronto should have a first-class orchestra and that we should hardly ever hear about it, let alone hear it." It was one of those statements which generates great pride in the arts-oriented Canadian, but which eventually settles into a melancholy query — 'Why didn't we think of that?' Salzman's comment embodies the entire issue of Canadian cultural promotion per se, a pivotal remark and question around which the Canadian careers of both Walter Susskind and Sheila revolved.

To counteract what he sensed was a basic lack of self-confidence amongst the local cultural establishment, Susskind founded the National Youth Orchestra, an organization devoted to the training of young musicians which also acted as a supply-source for all Canadian orchestras: individual training was one thing, but the chance to play in a large ensemble group, he felt, was invaluable to young musicians. The orchestra was an amazing success in its own right, above and beyond its service as a professional training ground. Audiences loved the youthful enthusiasm of its members and easily forgave any musical misdemeanors it committed in exchange for the rare gift of bubbling vitality.

Susskind loved Toronto, although he complained about the usual things conductors complained of: insufficient rehearsal time, union difficulties with regard to the hiring and firing of musicians, and the eternal bugbear, lack of funds. He was offered conducting jobs elsewhere, at more money, and turned them down for he felt Toronto was a lively and interesting city in which to live: in terms of the sweep of Toronto's general cultural life, he termed it far ahead of most cities on this continent.

"What an exhilerating city this is going to be, " he remarked, "when people understand just how alert, sophisticated and diversified a city they have and begin to take advantage of all the things that are here and press for more."

However, he encountered hostile reviews from music critics in the city, something he rarely had to contend with anywhere else in the world. John Kraglund of the *Globe and Mail,* in his summary of Susskind's term as TSO conductor, praised him for lifting the orchestra's morale to the highest level of its history then counterattacked by saying he was also responsible for depressing it to its nadir. Kraglund praised him for his great interpretive insight and condemned him, in the same sentence, for his superficiality. ("Susskind Will Leave Mixed Memories", *Globe and Mail*). In a soft-spoken rebuttal, Susskind believed that the Toronto press was, "addicted to looking negatively at things"; to emphasizing things of secondary importance. "When Herman Geiger-Torel introduces *Die Valkyrie* to Toronto, it is absurd that the main things the reviews should be taken up with is the quality of the scenery." Susskind, for his part, learned long ago to give critics the respect they deserve, "such as it is". But he pinned down the problem: a vicious cycle of lack of self-confidence, felt by the artists, fed to the community at large by the media, who fed it back to the performers via lack of support, a litany which continues to this day.

June, 1959, Bill had graduated from Pharmacy and the Henigs bought the couple a two-bedroom bungalow. Sheila felt settled and secure and began collecting, immediately, a menagerie of animals with Lassie, by virtue of tenure so to speak, occupying the place of honour. On June 15th she wrote to Carol: *I am very happy today. My parents bought us a two-bedroom bungalow! Bill has graduated this year and is working in a drug store. Everything is just great! I'll have to learn to cope with home responsibilities for the very first time.*

"For the very first time" would come only whenever there was free time which was becoming, blessedly, more and more infrequent in the last year of the '50s. She received a scholarship from the music publisher Frederick Harris to attend the master-classes of Soviet pianist Lev Oborin at the Stratford Festival during the summer. Professor Oborin, making his first North American appearance as both performer and teacher, was senior faculty member of the Moscow Conservatory of Music and had won both the Stalin and International Chopin prizes. And in what must have been a triumphant moment, Walter Susskind invited Sheila to play two nights with the Toronto Symphony in Massey Hall during the 1959-60 season on its major series. True, she had already appeared with the Symphony in the student and 'pop' series. These two back-to-back concerts, however, placed Sheila in the prime spotlight distinguished artists series, with her first concert being broadcast over CBC radio nationally. All this happened very quickly — the 'feast or famine' syndrome. Sheila was beginning to realize, as do all those who choose a life-work out of the mainstream employee-employer relationship, that this was something she would have to adjust to. There would be long periods without work where seemingly everything she had worked for was of "no value" to her society; then the offers would pour in.

It was up to each guest artist in the distinguished artists series to name the work of his or her choice, subject always to the approval of Susskind. Sheila, fascinated by the unfamiliar and adventurous, selected an obscure composition, Dvorak's *Piano Concerto*, for what would be its first Toronto, possibly its first Canadian, performance. The Czech composer, Anton Dvorak, played the piano, but indifferently. He was far happier performing on the violin, viola and cello. He composed a potentially effective, and affecting, concerto for piano but the keyboard part was so ungrateful that the work soon passed into oblivion. It was written after the composer lost his daughter; it was romantic, big in scale, and the drama of the father's anguish came through, particularly in the first two movements. A modern Czech scholar took it up and with integrity and skill, revised the piano part so that it was more substantial, brilliant and playable. He passed this revision along to his star pupil, pianist Rudolf Firkusny, who recorded it. Sheila heard this recording one night as she was listening to the radio; the next day she bought the only copy of the score available in Toronto and began to study it in earnest. When she offered it for Susskind's approval, he was delighted.

Toronto, however, would not be the premiere city in Canada for this rarely heard showpiece. That honour would go 3,000 miles away to the most old-English atmosphere city in Canada, Victoria, B.C. Sheila felt more secure with an "out of town tryout" as she put it.

Situated on the lush green temperate hills of Vancouver Island overlooking the Pacific, British Columbia's capital city is a charming reminder of an earlier, more gracious era when the sun would never set over the Empire. Victoria's mood was light-years away from the hip West Coast futuristic sophistication of Vancouver; neither did it reflect the nascent trendiness of London. It was, rather, a mood representing the timeless ideal of Queen and afternoon tea promptly at four o'clock. It was also a mood conducive to a deep appreciation of classical music. For a city of only 165,000, Victorian had a remarkably good orchestra in 1959 under the leadership of German-Jewish refugee, Hans Gruber. On November 8, Sheila was guest-performer. Victoria took Sheila to its heart and loved the Dvorak work. Audrey Johnson of the *Victoria Daily Times* reviewed —

> . . . This young Canadian proved to be a most musicianly pianist. Her approach is serious and dedicated to a degree that, even in the most

spectacular passages of a truly virtuoso work, she appeared to emphasize and draw her audience's attention to its underlying musical properties.

She has a sympathetic touch that produces a consistently lovely tone. An authoritative and fluent technique is intelligently disciplined by good taste. This was virtuosity expressed gracefully and not — as is too often the case — empty of mind and heart.

She also received an unusually warm, loving letter from the secretary of the Victoria Symphony Society:

Dear Miss Henig,
One of the privileges of being a secretary to a Symphony Society is having contact with artists whom, otherwise, I would look at from an audience point of view. I am fortunate enough to sometimes get a chance of seeing the artist as he or she really is — as we did last evening at Mrs. Milburn's. It was an opportunity I shall cherish — to watch one of our outstanding pianists become "one of the party" and give us entertainment of the highest calibre; and then "turn the pages" for the trio. It all made the "star" shine more brightly — you will always have a warm welcome in Victoria.

God bless you always in what I know is now, and will be, a successful career.

(Miss) E.S. McGillivray
Secretary.

Sheila had already responded to the warmth of Victoria before even receiving Miss McGillivray's letter. "Thank you, Victoria, B.C.", she wrote. It was obvious the experience had been a great one for her. "I was feeling great and confident both nights, I couldn't wait to get on stage and give it my best. I think that the act of appreciation and kindness that was bestowed on me by music V.I.P.'s upon my arrival, and the reception given in my honour the day of the concert, added a great deal to the successful performances. I was overwhelmingly pleased with both. It was quite an experience. Some characters in the audience kept on screaming, 'More! More!', the ushers couldn't shut them up. Thank you, wherever you are. I appreciate recognition, doesn't everyone?" (October 27, 1959).

Two days later, she pleaded with Carol to answer her letters.

(October 29th, 1959)

Dear Carol,
Enclosed you'll find two interviews that appeared in the Toronto and Victoria newspapers. I was delighted to read them especially the one in the Victoria Daily Times. It makes it all worthwhile.
I'm concerned about you, I haven't heard from you in ages.

Perhaps you are disturbed that I write a lot about myself? If you are, please tell me, but what are friends for? I wish you would write dozens of pages to me, instead of being evasive on so many things including your personal problems. Don't hesitate to tell me, we have been friends for so long we should therefore confide in each other. It's easier to cope with life when you can share it with a friend. I'm on a high now but that doesn't mean I can't share with you if your life isn't going the same. You have been such a big help to me in the past, when you've "listened" to me, through my letters and if I've misused you that way, I'm sorry. I keep up a front sometimes, at home, amongst my family and friends, because I feel it's expected of me — or maybe I expect it of myself, I don't know which. But once I opened that door with you, it's alright with me — and you've never complained.

Please, please write me soon, tell me how you are. Don't disappoint me.

Love,
Sheila

Sheila felt confident the Dvorak concerto would be at least an equal success in Toronto. Morris Duff's interview (*Toronto Star,* January 5, 1960), heralding her spotlight appearance with the Toronto Symphony (January 5-6, '60) was warm and friendly touching on the personal and musical; Sheila wanted to talk about the Dvorak work. "I'm always in the market for something different and this was a beautiful thing." Sheila continued, "We hear the same old warhorses all the time. The time has come for us to get things that are different. And the wonderful thing about this concerto is that it is not modern. It is as romantic as Tchaikovsky." Duff asked her about the Victoria performance of the piece: "The audience, made up of ordinary people, loved it," Sheila reported. "I believe it is a work with great appeal to the layman. Of course, I will have another test here in Toronto. The audience is a bit more sophisticated. It's a better orchestra. So, we'll see?"

Morris Duff continued with the more personal, light human-interest aspects.

Sheila puts her child prodigy act in spelling down to a good memory. "I could remember what my mother told me so I could spell words like 'Mississippi'. That was at the time of the Shirley Temple craze. I was a contralto if you can imagine a three-year-old contralto.

"At four I was a tap dancer so my parents decided to take me to Hollywood. I auditioned for Eddie Cantor. He said I was talented but to take me home from the rat race and let me grow up normally. I think that was pretty good advice.

"I thought everybody had forgotten that," Sheila said, when asked about the time she entered the Miss Canada Contest [as a teenager]. "I entered for

the talent end of the contest but found I had to go through the whole bit —
bathing suits and all. Actually the contest is a farce, but it wasn't a waste of
time. I learned how to put on make-up and walk like a model.

"But I don't believe in beauty contests. I think their values are wrong.
Girls parade around like a bunch of cattle. And they measure you. It's all
very degrading."

She explained she married former Olympic boxer Bill Sidney because
she's "mad about athletes" even though "I'm terribly unathletic".

Sheila had to give up skating for fear of falling and hurting an arm. Tennis
went because it caused blisters on her thumbs.

All this doesn't mean Sheila wanders around fearful of hurting her hands,
like Glenn Gould. "I have none of Glenn's mannerisms. I wear gloves in the
winter, but why do you need them when it's warm out?

"I think it's a psychological problem," Sheila said of the famous Gould
antics.

"But music is a very personal thing. I don't sleep well the night before a
concert and I have to take a special kind of sleeping pill. The music keeps
running through my head. I play the entire concerto from beginning to end.
By that time, I'm dizzy."

Sheila's performance with the Toronto Symphony was the most triumphant
so far. She felt she excelled herself; Susskind was ecstatic with the performance
of the Dvorak work and with the audience's response to it. Enthusiasm ran very
high on the nights of January 5 and 6 and the critics damned the performance.
Among her professional associates at the time was Stuart Hamilton, another
pianist who, although an acclaimed soloist in New York and London, was
specializing in accompanying opera singers. (Today he is founder-director of a
unique organization, Opera in Concert, in Toronto, which gives opera singers a
chance to perform full-length operas without the expenses of a full-scale
production; his accompanying led to very good ends indeed.) At the time, Stuart
was already an erudite and critical observer of the international music scene,
and he thought Sheila's performance of the Concerto was marvellous —
"Beautiful!" he enthused to her in her dressing room. The harsh criticism
levelled at Sheila was beyond everybody's comprehension, including Susskind's.

Fortunately for Sheila, Susskind's sense of perspective, and most important of all, his own self-confidence in his intuitive feelings of what was excellent,
was not swayed by the negative reviews. He was due to guest-conduct the
Houston Symphony the following month and he was determined to feature her
as star soloist — again, performing the Dvorak Concerto.

Even at that time, Houston was America's city of the future; it's future
today is perhaps a bit dubious for it owes its prosperity to Arab oil money and its
vassals, the major American oil companies. Then, however, the Houston boom
was mostly in the aerospace industry. It was a rambunctious, optimistic city
which embraced both Sheila and Susskind in the wonderful Texan tradition of
expansive, effervescent acceptance. Her bold decision to choose, learn and
perform — and then to stand by it — the Dvorak work was immediately

recognized by Houston symphony goers; they gave her their full measure of approval. Sheila herself wrote about the experience — whether she was intending to mail it in the form of a letter, or have it published in Toronto, no one knows.

I owe a vote of thanks to conductor Walter Susskind for inviting me to play as guest artist with the Houston Symphony Orchestra. The audience accepted me with open arms and expressed their appreciation before, during and after the concert. I'm also grateful to the critics of the Houston Press *and the Houston* Post *for their kind reviews. That particular concert was very important to me because it was conducted by Mr. Susskind, whom I admire as a sensitive person.*

My memories of Houston will always be connected with the snow which fell while we were there. The temperature had dropped forty degrees overnight when we arrived and it snowed. There was great excitement among the members of the orchestra and, of course, we were kidded about bringing the snow from Canada in our suitcases.

That unforgettable evening, everything seemed to go my way. The piano was well-tuned and responded beautifully to my touch. The huge audience was most enthusiastic and contributed a great deal to one of my best performances in memory. A good appreciative audience brings out the best in an artist. It gives you confidence which comes through the tips of your fingers. It's exciting, satisfying and almost hypnotic.

Critics are, as a rule, very hard on artists. They seem to find fault with the most trivial incidents, like a slip of a finger or the manipulation of a piano pedal. Very seldom do they give the artist the praise he or she deserves. I sometimes think that they are getting paid for being mean. However, their criticism doesn't seem to bother me anymore. It's the reaction of the audience that counts. On this occasion, both the critics and the audience were in agreement on the calibre of my performance.

(February, 1960)

What was all the fuss about? What did the Texans have to say about Sheila and Walter Susskind? They had much to say about these two, and Toronto itself, the wealth of existing talent which the city produces. Ann Holmes, Fine Arts Editor of the Houston *Chronicle* asked: "What do they feed musicians in Toronto, anyway?" A key question, indeed. Sheila had no answer. "It's just one of those things," she finally said in answer to Miss Holmes query. "For a long time, Toronto has been producing strong talent. At long last the world of music is beginning to recognize it." The reviews have been lost or misplaced from Sheila's belongings; what remains are 'blurbs' recopied for a concert promotion sheet. The Houston *Post*: "She is a musician, bless her, and the audience brought her back five times to acknowledge its honours — a thoroughly fine, fluent, expressive technique — perceives the poetry in the musical line — rare sweetness and lustre of tone throughout." The *Press* said: (in capsule form) "Her technique is dazzling — pours in a great affection for her music — She is destined to become one of the great keyboard artists."

Once she got back home, George Kidd, music critic of the *Toronto Telegram*, gave Sheila a rave review on her rave reviews!

Texas Loves Our Musicians.
The Houston Chronicle Wonders . . .
Down Texas way they're trying to figure out what Toronto feeds its musicians and how they progress so well under the guidance of conductor Walter Susskind.
A week ago Toronto pianist Sheila Henig played with the Houston Symphony Orchestra, with Mr. Susskind on the podium.
The three newspapers came forth the next day with rave reviews and two of them commented on the wealth of talent that exists here.

And so on. A blunt about-face. No mention was made of the reviews given Sheila for a similar performance in Toronto.

Sheila joined many of Toronto's talent for the Easter Parade of Stars, held in Maple Leaf Gardens, a great barn of a place designed for hockey, in benefit of the Canadian Council for Crippled Children and Adults, co-sponsored by Toronto's broadcasting industry. In the fall she went back to Victoria and drew headlines: "Pianist in Second Triumph with Victoria's Symphony" (*Victoria Daily Times*) and "Dynamic Music Displays Genius of Young Pianist" (Victoria Colonist), both dated October 24, 1960. Her second appearance in the city was as swamped with unconditional support as her first appearance. The program included Beethoven's seldom played *Piano Concert No. 1 in C minor,* Mozart's *'Linz' Symphony (No. 36),* William Walton's *Coronation March, "Crown Imperials"* and Brahm's *Variations on Haydn's St. Antoni Chorale.*

Sheila was in a gloriously optimistic mood, paralleling the upbeat, regenerative mood that was the beginning of the '60s'. No one knew at that time, of course, that "the '60s' " would be the clarion call of the 20th century, frought with demonstrations and disorder, but also an almost utopian belief that the human race could, if the '60s' would just go far enough, turn itself around and take control of the frightening array of destructive forces facing it. John F. Kennedy's "New Frontier" was the catchword — in America and Canada. The American voters had turfed out the tired, stuffy Eisenhower-Nixon legacy and voted in their first Catholic president. The popular mood was hip, frenetically futuristic and youth-oriented: the Twist was the number one dance craze; fashions reflected the sleek, youthfully sophisticated image of the new American First Lady, Jacqueline Bouvier Kennedy — and Sheila was on her way to conquer the opposite side of the Atlantic, starting with Geneva.

Mr. Arnold Walter, President of the International Society of Music suggested that Sheila register for the Geneva International Competition to take place in September, 1961. The necessary application and recommendations were mailed and Sheila was accepted. But on July 23, 1961 as Sheila was preparing for the competition, her mother suffered a massive brain hemmorhage which reduced her to the 'human vegetable' state. Sheila, emotionally intense at the best of times, was shattered. She wrote a note — or the beginning of a letter, it was never finished — in an attempt to rationalize her very difficult dilemma. *I have worked hard, practicing six to eight hours a day, preparing for this most important competition of my career. I know that I can win first prize. I can feel it in my bones and now, now that I am confronted with this tragedy, how can I possibly leave for Geneva when my mother is so gravely ill?*

Although she is unaware of my presence, I know that I belong here; but if I don't show, a year of hard, back-breaking work will be wasted.

In an intensely confused state, she decided to go; Bill would accompany her. He was emotionally strong, and there was still the solidness and discipline of the athlete about him. If anybody could help her through it, he could do it.

When she arrived in Geneva she was physically and emotionally exhausted. She describes it herself: *I sat down at the piano, my mind was a thousand miles away. I was in a daze, I had one hell of a headache and kept thinking, I shouldn't be here. I somehow managed to get through, more by instinct than concentration. Then I was told the following day that I had made the finals — and then, at the end of it all, I won the Laureate. I don't know how I did it.*

The beauty and tranquility of the Swiss countryside and mountains had a great leveling effect on her; they continued to Amsterdam where she was scheduled for a concert in the recital hall of the famed Concertgebouw, unquestionably a very important one for her because it was her first European appearance and hopefully, there would be important reviews to relay back to the hometown press. A translation of one of them is given in its entirety.

PIANO DEBUT IN AMSTERDAM, HOLLAND
Concertgebouw, Small Hall
PRESS NOTICES
Het Parool — October 23, 1961
Sheila Henig — A Great Musician

The name of Sheila Henig is one to remember — this we understood immediately when we heard her debut in the Small Hall of the Concertgebouw. A great musician from whose fingers, without any demonstrative passion, comes a very colourful, attention-capturing expression. Her "toucher" is always clean and round and her use of the pedal is exceptional and very much related to the demands of the music. She started Ravel's "Sonatine" a little slower than we are used to, but this was justified as it gained in expressive mood. In the closing Anime of this work and in

Chopin's "Fantasie (OP. 49)" she showed a virtuosity and a flawless technique. Apropos, we have seldom heard the coda of the Fantasie played as intensely as at this time. "Les Funerailles" by Liszt was played with volume and overwhelming power. Two preludes by Rachmaninoff were given full justice to detail and a great musical temperament was shown in her playing. It is for certain that the pianist sometimes plays too slowly, but even then the details sound so honest and well balanced that one can listen and be satisfied. An unforgettable experience was her encore "Feux Follets" by I. Philipp where she showed a "cobwebby", glittering facility.

Leo Hoost

Other Dutch music critics, considered "the most difficult to impress in Europe" (CBC Times, Nov. 9-15/63) described her performance as "faultless virtuosity . . . real romanticism in the most sensitive and impassioned way . . . ardent, tender and deeply serious." Another remark in this CBC Times article, announcing her performance with the CBC Symphony Orchestra conducted by Alexander Brott (November 10, 1963) stated that, "One of her unrealized ambitions is to be invited back to Winnipeg for a concert or recital. She has never had the opportunity of playing the piano professionally in her birthplace."

Good reviews from Europe is nothing but good news for Canadian artists in their home country. Shortly after her return, Sheila performed with the Atlantic Orchestra of Halifax as part of its Summer Music Festival under the direction of John Fenwick. She again played the Beethoven *Piano Concerto No. 1 in C minor* which had been such a hit in Victoria, Chopin's *Fantasia in F minor* and some short pieces by Brahms and Debussy. For the CBC concert in November, Sheila was, once more, adventurous in her selection of repertoire and she gave a spectacular performance of Bela Bartok's *Rhapsody for Piano and Orchestra*, a dynamically challenging fusion of Hungarian folk melodies and contemporary semi-abstraction.

Twelve days later John F. Kennedy was assassinated. By the following summer, America was into the depths of her Vietnam mess and Sheila was about to embark upon what was to become the crown jewel of her career: her second trip to Europe, and her first, real European tour (November-December, 1964).

That trip was a collage of so many incredible events — exciting, amusing and not-so-amusing — that it's hard to know where to begin.

So wrote Sheila, summing up her tour — a true triumph when, in November of 1964, she won the hearts of audiences and music elite in Greece, Austria, Spain and London.

I'll begin at the first stop, Greece, which was a wonderful place to start the tour — the people being so warm and hospitable. When the plane door opened [Athens airport] and I was about to descend, I saw a red carpet at the bottom (on the tarmac) and someone holding a large bouquet of flowers with a photographer. I naturally assumed there was a celebrity on the plane, but it was for me — *a complete stranger to them. I've never had such treatment in Canada.*

There were more delightful surprises in store. First, the reporters interviewed her on the spot, something usually reserved for Prime Ministers and movie stars in Canada. The pre-concert interviews were published the very next day, and all of them were prefaced with such banner phrases as, "A GREAT CANADIAN PIANIST IN ATHENS", "The internationally famous Canadian pianist...", "The famous artist..." They reported what the activities of the star and her husband would be, apart from concerts, while they were in Greece. They were warmly appreciative of the lovely things Sheila said about Greece, Greek music and musicians. Once they left the airport, Sheila was treated to an even more astounding experience... *There were huge yellow six-foot posters announcing my performances plastered on every second lamp-post*... she exclaimed in wonder. *I couldn't believe it!* She loved the movement and colour of the Athens' streets and said so to anybody who would listen to her; the Greeks responded with delight.

To receive such treatment anywhere, for any performer, is very special and unforgettable. But to receive such treatment in Greece was even more exceptional, in Sheila's mind. She was deeply impressed with the sense of timelessness, the merging of past and present, that is the heritage of Greece — *the incredible scenic splendour of the coastline and the mountains, and then to look at, and walk into, the ancient structures of the Acropolis and the Parthenon,* which to Sheila symbolized the beginning of the democratic tradition and artistic civilization.

The glory of Greece lives on, she wrote later. *Anybody who has been to Greece will tell you that!*

Her tour in the country was being handled by George P. Kourakos of the Bureau Artistique d'Athènes; the reception, throughout the country, was due to his very careful advance publicity, tapping into the natural Greek ebullience for the arts and their delight in anything that promises a sublime experience. She was due to play at Athens' Gloria Theatre on November 9; on the 6th and 7th there were recitals in the northern Greek towns of Patras and Agrinion. After she and Bill had visited the Acropolis and a few museums, her tour began — a long bus ride through mountainous roads into the northern part of Greece, where she gave the first and second of her scheduled three concerts. All of the concerts featured the same program: Liszt, Schumann, Debussy and Prokofieff. Although the pianos left something to be desired in both towns, the audiences were warmly receptive and enthusiastic — *I'll never forget the big feast they treated us to in Patras after my concert.* And then, on a beautiful Monday evening, she gave her major concert in the heart of Athens. The reviews were ecstatic: (The originals in Greek have been lost. These are translations of excerpts, unfortunately not very good ones)

Pianists, pianists — never have we heard so many artists of the 'King of organs'. And here is another pianist sent to us from Canada; Miss SHEILA HENIG whom we heard Monday at the *Gloria* one hour before the concert of the National Orchestra. Sure technique, rich sounds — a little strong in the 'forte' — clear musicality and concert interpretation of the spirit. These are the qualities of Miss Henig. She started her program with the Sonata #2 in D Minor by Prokofieff which she played with sentiment and expression. She continued with the Fantaisiestucke of Schumann. Here, Miss Henig specially showed her musicality and sensitivity. It was a beautiful, sentimental and poetical interpretation.

. . . .

Alexandra Lalouni, Vradyni

The Canadian pianist Sheila Henig we heard on Monday is a great artist. She opened the program with the Sonata #2 by Prokofieff. Miss Henig proved how well she knows how to "build" the music, to give sequence in the changes of tempos and interpret, with clarity and musicality, the difficult technical parts. . . . .

Mesimvrini

. . . .

This young pianist . . . has excellent musical qualities. Sure technique, understanding of the style of the playing she interprets, delicate sentiment, rhythm and exactness: in view of all this her interpretation leaves a deep impression.

Wonderful was the interpretation of the Sonata of Prokofieff; a very high artistic level in the Fantaisiestucke. The two parts of the Suite of Debussy combined the beauty of the sound and poetical fantasies. . . .

Jean Gianoulis, Ethnikos Kiryx

She was called back for four encores. The following day, "this distinguished virtuose" (*Ethnos*) performed over the Greek National Radio, and the day following gave another recital (unscheduled) at Philothei. She had scored a great triumph "out front"; she scored an equally tremendous personal triumph in the less spectacular, but ultimately more important arena of "behind the scenes". Mr. Kouraskis was more than satisfied with the outcome of the tour — which would mean further tours. "Not only did we present an artist with a great future in front of her, but a lady of great simplicity, which in our work we seldom meet." On the Sunday before the Athens concert, they all went to a party at the home of Dascoulis, a famous Greek pianist, where the guests were "of the best society", according to Mr. Kourakis. He quoted, in this letter to Sheila's manager at the time, Aladar Ecsedy of Daniel Attractions (Hamilton, Ontario), Mrs. Alexandra Lalaounis, influential music critic of *Vradyni* — "Sheila Henig is a real discovery and must be put in value." Sheila herself wrote: *I cried when I left Athens, I had become so fond of that wonderful man, George Kourakis, who had arranged all my concerts. I was never to know that kind of personal care and warmth during the remainder of my tour.* They had time to sample a bit of Athens' fabulous, non-stop swinging nightlife, whose cafes and restaurants ring all night to the sounds of Greek folk music performed by singing dancers, accompanied by bouzoukis. Even in November, Sheila felt that the city seemed to be overrun with U.S. and Canadian tourists.

When we arrived in Vienna, we went to visit the man who was arranging my Austrian tour (I was to play in Salzburg, Graz and Vienna), and I had a rude shock. It seems there was some mix-up in financial arrangements between my Canadian manager and this gentleman. He threatened to cancel all three concerts if the matter wasn't cleared up by next morning! My heart stopped, but I didn't panic! I called my manager in Canada and had him straighten everything out at once. It wasn't a great introduction to Austria, but everything was uphill from there on.

There was no red-carpet welcome at the Vienna airport, but Austria had other compensations.

Vienna remains one of the most rigorous testing grounds for classical musicians. Throughout the country audiences and critics are very knowledgeable and their standards are very high. Students attend concerts as a regular course and usually they are given free tickets. They bring the scores of the pieces to be played. *It is somewhat unnerving to hear the rustle of pages turning together. You know they're watching and listening to every note!*

Sheila's first concert, in Graz, resulted in eight curtain calls and three encores. It also inspired one listener to drag her husband to Vienna for the pianist's recital a few days later. In Salzburg, whose best known homegrown talent is Mozart, the manager of the hall, the small but famous Mozarteum, said it was the best piano recital of the season and he phoned the concert hall in Vienna to relay the news. According to the local newspaper, the large audience "experienced an outwardly attractive personality" who was "able to demonstrate a markedly modern culture of expression with power and technique".

Vienna was the ultimate test and Sheila seemed to pass it with top marks; one major critic suggested they should bring her back — "It would be a welcome enrichment to our concert life" — a statement not to be shrugged off lightly. He also praised her performance saying she was "able to give an excellent impression with her faultless interpretations." Later, the Austrian impressario wrote to the Canadian Embassy in Vienna, and to Ottawa, to say it had been a long time since an unknown musician had made so big an impression in Vienna. Sheila was happy indeed — *All my Austrian reviews were excellent and that meant a lot coming from those critics.*

From a strictly musical viewpoint, what was most particularly remarkable about Sheila's Vienna concert was that she opened it with a complete stylistic departure from her usual repertoire: Bach's *G-minor Prelude and Fugue*. As stated before, she rarely performed unarranged Bach, for she hadn't felt comfortable with the stylized grace necessary to perform it, or with the meticulousness of the music form. She preferred what one friend called, "the grand panoramic overview", music that mirrored her own passionate intensity and wilfullness. It is interesting that she chose this work to perform in what would probably be her most difficult city to conquer, musically. Possibly she felt she owed the musical heritage that belongs to Vienna a burst of emotional discipline on her part. Regardless of her reasons, she was successful, and unquestionably pleased that she had made this step into new musical experiences for herself. The remainder of the Vienna concert included the Schumann, Prokofieff and Liszt works which had proven to be such a success in Greece.

A brief holiday in Paris for Sheila and Bill followed the Vienna concert; it provided an opportunity to hear Russian pianist, Sviatoslav Richter, with conductor Lorin Maazel, in a special concert at the Paris Opera. Afterwards, he told Sheila that his Toronto recital had been a "dreadful performance".

Spain was next on the itinerary, and this part of the tour was such a fiasco — probably what she was referring to when she remarked on "not-so-amusing" events — that it is best told in Sheila's own words.

From Paris, we flew to Madrid amid some feelings of apprehension. While in Paris, I called the manager in Madrid who was to look after my tour of Spain. He was never in, so I thought we'd better get there and find out what was going on. When we finally saw the manager (after a two-hour wait because he was out to lunch), we found him very charming but also very vague about my tour. Nothing had yet been arranged — not even my "big" Madrid concert (I was under the impression that I was playing there the following week). This "manana" attitude was in such great contrast to the super-efficiency of the Austrians that I'm afraid I never did get used to it. The tour was finally organized, but there was no advertising, and what's more, we had to keep in constant touch with London to change a BBC recital date which had been previously scheduled and which now had to be rescheduled due to the seemingly chaotic booking arrangements in Spain.

But at last we were off — off to the northern part of Spain where it is very cold in December. The concert in the first town, Palencia, was not too bad. The piano was barely playable; I think I could have gotten a nicer sound from a desk.

The next concert in Zamora was the low-point of my entire tour. There was, of course, a communication problem. I didn't speak Spanish and they didn't speak English (this was a problem that plagued us even in Madrid). I had hoped someone would speak French, but no luck. When I arrived at the hall, which was an auditorium in a school, it was bitterly cold. We tried to explain, as best we could, that they must do something about the heat before the evening's concert and we got the idea that they understood us. However, when I arrived for the concert the hall was still freezing. It was so cold that we could see our breath backstage!

We stalled for a while, trying to find the janitor. He just shrugged his shoulders. Finally, I had to start, unfortunately wearing a sleeveless dress and no sweater to put over it (my coat was too bulky). How I ever played that evening I will never know. At intermission, out of desperation, my husband Bill went looking for the furnace and found it directly under the stage. There was no fire going, so Bill started chopping wood and started a fire in the furnace. I couldn't put off the second half any longer. So, with wood-chopping going on underneath me I started to play Debussy. I can never play the Clair de Lune now without thinking of that incident. Just to top it off, I was playing on the worst piano I had yet encountered. I knew from the rehearsal what I would be up against. There were at least three keys that went down and refused to come up unless they were pushed up. So, throughout the entire concert, I had to remember which keys they were so that I could release them immediately after playing them. Also, the piano had a squeaky pedal and it decided to go travelling across the stage with me trying to keep up by moving the bench at every opportunity. I eventually ended the concert almost off-stage. An absolute nightmare! I might add, the hall started to warm up (with Bill furiously stoking the furnace) by the end of the program. I was sure I was going to catch pneumonia that night and was very worried because the all-important London concert was less than a week away.

We had decided to take a train that passed through the town at 3 a.m. so we could get back to Madrid and rest before my concert there, after this ordeal. At the hotel they informed us that there were no taxis running at that hour of the night but they did offer us a young boy to help carry our bags to the station. There we were, the three of us, trudging down the main street of Zamora, on a cold middle-of-the-night to the train station. When the train arrived we thought — at last, we'll be warm! — but that was not to be. Out of all the compartments, we managed to choose one whose heater wasn't working. So, half-frozen and sleepless, we arrived back in Madrid, mid-morning.

In retrospect, it all seems quite amusing. But at the time, I assure you, it was not.

I recuperated in time for my Madrid concert two days later. I cannot say whether it was a success or not (I know my encore, a piece by Gravados, brought many bravos) because there were no critics present due to lack of publicity. There was an American pianist in the audience (whose name I can't remember; a pupil of Rudolf Serkin) who was on tour and came backstage to congratulate me after the concert. He seemed very impressed and moved by my playing and particularly impressed by the way I handled the "monster" Steinway piano. It was an excellent piano (in contrast to others I had to use during my tour) but it was very heavy and difficult to manage, and it was notorious among touring pianists.

Prior to departing Spain, we did some sightseeing in Toledo and saw ancient Jewish synagogues dating back to pre-Inquisition times.

London was the last and perhaps the most important stop because a Wigmore Hall debut is comparable to a New York Town Hall debut in America. *Even the weather was nice,* Sheila said, *and I had a good crowd at the concert.* She also saw some familiar Canadian faces in her dressing-room afterwards.

Strangely enough, Sheila wrote, *I wasn't particularly nervous for this all-important concert. Perhaps everything I had been through up until that point made me impervious to anxiety. I played well and received a standing ovation, which, coming from the so-called "cool" British audience was totally unexpected. My concert was on the pre-Christmas Saturday (December 19, 1964) and we were leaving for home the following day so I did not see any reviews. Because it was close to Christmas and the manager had neglected to send the reviews by first-class mail, I waited two weeks (which seemed like two years!). The two main papers were there and the reviews were both good:* the Telegraph *hailed* "vivacious pianist — striking — great sensitivity — splendid and compelling"; *the* Times *described my playing as* "the heroic and the poetic — a nobility of utterance near the grand manner — revealing a dexterity more than equal to the challenge of her program — energetic and expressive". *People who know the* Times *told me that this was pratically a rave coming from that paper.*

Immediately after her Wigmore Hall debut, Sheila performed over the BBC, which was broadcast on short wave reaching South America, Europe, North America and Africa, and then on the Home Service.

Summed up, from the red carpet and flowers of the Athens airport to performing within view of the Acropolis; within the small fabled parlour in Salzburg where Mozart himself premiered his works to Vienna; from the wild adventure in wintry northern Spain to the sophistication of London music critics, Sheila Henig's first European concert tour was a wonderful success. The experience itself was invaluable — and occassionally, abysmal — and it provided the opportunity to collect the obligatory European reviews, which should then guarantee a few rave remarks from the hometown media people.

Only two major papers — and those, of course, were in Toronto — gave any notice at all that Sheila had either been away or returned with a suitcase full of good reviews. The *Globe and Mail* published a low-key interview report by music critic John Kraglund which, although providing a fairly detailed and accurate account of the physical details of the trip, failed to mention any of the pieces she performed and did not emphasize the reception of audiences and critics. It headlined the article with a bit of tacky trivia, musically anyway, "Tour Featured Wood Chopping, Sticky Keys". The *Toronto Telegram* served her better. Headlined, "Sheila Is Back — Europe Loved Her", music critic George Kidd wrote: "Toronto pianist Sheila Henig has returned home from an European tour with her hands filled with excellent reviews and a perplexed look on her attractive face.

She wonders why she has not been given more opportunities to appear in Canada. She has never appeared in her own hometown, Winnipeg, and neither has she performed in Vancouver. Montreal has never requested her presence.

In Toronto, she has fared better, giving numerous recitals and appearing with the Toronto Symphony. Recently, in fact, she had to turn down a local offer with the orchestra because of the tour, which included eleven concerts and several broadcasts in Greece, Australia, Spain and London, and a brief holiday in Paris with her husband William Sidney.

"I certainly can't complain about the chances I have been given in Toronto," said the former winner of the coveted Eaton Award. "I've appeared with the CBC and toured to various spots in Ontario. But the major cities seem to give me the cold shoulder."

January 11, 1965

George Kidd amplified on the European critical and audience triumphs and listed her previous successes. The interview closed with remarks from Sheila — "This last tour, which was made possible by Daniel Attractions, came at a time when I was becoming discouraged! (said Miss Henig) This has happened to so many artists in the past, but some of them have been persistent and finally succeeded. But I would like to play in my own country."

She expressed her discouragement in a letter to Carol (March 18, 1965) *... I came back with a heart full of hope that perhaps even in Canada there is still opportunity for artists like myself to be recognized in our own country, rather than have to travel to Europe to seek recognition.*

I don't mean to imply that I haven't been given the opportunity to perform in Canada. In fact, I'm extremely grateful for everything Canada has done for me. I am, however, getting a bit tired of knocking on doors, after hammering away on the piano for thirty years for six to eight hours a day. One certainly gets discouraged sometimes when things don't come your way as you think they should. I'm sadly aware that the competition is fierce, but how many times does a performer have to prove him-her-self? I had really expected more upon my return than what I got. But thank God for small mercies. I consider myself fortunate that I don't have to depend on my career for a living.

I have been trying to capture dreams most of my life, and succeeded to some extent. I'm satisfied to have had the opportunity of catching some which became reality and to be recognized as a first-class performer. I have paid a high price for my measure of success, of course, but it was all worth it.

Give my best to Peter.

Love,
Sheila.

It was now the mid-60s and if any of us remember — how could we forget — the "greening of America" was in full swing, consciousness-raising was the international pastime, and Canada, to its everlasting credit, took in hordes of American draft-dodgers and deserters. Any state of mind you wanted was obtainable from a drug (illegal); those who didn't chose this particular alternative lifestyle, went to psychiatrists who were buying bigger and better homes. Looked back upon from the '80s, it was a time of almost nirvana; certainly it is remembered with warmth and nostalgia. It was a decade of abuse and some wonderful break-throughs in putting our house in order in terms of righting social wrongs. It spawned a kind of permissiveness which said, "I'm Okay, You're Okay" and a lot of old conventions were thrown away. There was also Expo '67 and Canada would never be as self-confident again.

Canadians erupted in a burst of nationalism, a bit self-consciously perhaps at first, but there was a hopefulness that the spirit of "Canadians first" would catch on. The artistic community generally — music, art, theatre, dance, literature — caught on to the initial enthusiasm (particularly theatre and dance for they had been the underdogs of the community till then; writers would have to wait even longer for their Can-Lit credo, but when it came it was heavy-duty) and began to spread their wings. The Canada Council was developed as a state-patronage agency for the arts. Life looked promising indeed.

But there was another, more global element developing, culturally, at the same time. Like a gangling adolescent, the Canadian media, hungry for an instant separate-identity model, seized upon the youth counterculture and, in a manner comparable to fringe-underground publications everywhere, embraced it as an embryo for a new Canadian identity, utilizing Stokely Carmichael's "Black Power" and Quebec separatist forms of national socialism as models after which to fashion a new "Canadian cultural nationalism". Initially, this new "youth-trendy" spirit differed little from the hippie-exuberance of San Francisco's Haight-Ashbury, New York's East Village or London's Chelsea. Yorkville in Toronto compared favourably with, and eventually overtook, its other bohemian counterparts. And as long as the Vietnam war was on, this spirit seemed preferable to the right-wing jingoism which had precipitated the war. From the beginning, this new "hip" media spirit, especially in Toronto, contained cultural preferences which, in order to most closely identify with the "masses", favoured folk-agrarianism over urban-cosmopolitanism. These preferences were the legacy of the American folk-hero Bob Dylan. Canadian folk singers, rock'n' rollers, and "back-alley" government-grant theatres were to benefit most in terms of media coverage, and thus, inevitably, popular recognition, but many of these groups tended to disappear as quickly as they appeared. They were not known for their perseverence or longevity. Classical music, which continued to be funded generously by the Councils, particularly where it pertained to community efforts, did not receive the same kind of hot-line star-making treatment in the media. It did not fare as well, in spite of the new cultural enlightenment.

On May 25, 1965, Sheila wrote Carol, telling her about the baby girl she and Bill had just adopted. *I now have a darling little girl. She has sky-blue eyes, blonde hair, and adorable face and a dimple in each cheek. She is two weeks old and her name is Shawna. I can't even begin to tell you how happy we are. When I hold her in my arms, I can hear angels sing and I'm at peace with myself and the world.*

I'm aware of the fact that I'll have to turn down European tours, and although I have a girl in the house helping me, I wouldn't think of leaving my little Shawna for the sake of a concert tour. I'll be happy to devote to her as much of my time as possible, instead of concertizing. I will perform close to home, provided my absence is no more than a day or two. I never believed that having a child could bring such overwhelming happiness to us. Our house has become a real home which we enjoy every minute of each day.

July 5, l965.
Dear Sheila,

I know I owe you an apology for not answering your letters, but when you have read my note, you'll understand.

As you know, my marriage to Peter has been happy, so much so that I haven't felt any need to talk about it. We moved to Calgary as planned. My father sold the farm and moved to Vancouver, and Scott is living with him for the time being. Peter and I have lived quietly but with great happiness until a few months ago, when my leg began bothering me again and I was told by my doctor that an infection is gradually setting in. I can't put in words how devastated I am — my hopes for a normal life have been shattered. I'll write you again just as soon as I can, but for now I don't feel like saying much to anybody. Keep well and take care.

Love, Carol

Sheila was heartbroken for her friend and wrote her several times again. But she would never hear from Carol again.

The latter half of the sixties were exciting years for Canadians, reaching a fever pitch in the '67 Centennial Year celebrations. Canadian artists and performers were grandstanding all over the country; suddenly the "performer" was in demand, for it was the performer who could help create the environment that would bring the masses together. There was an enormous amount of ethnic performing activity; Canada was celebrating, to coin a phrase, her "vertical mosaic". The country's professionals were looked upon in a new light, they were assets to the country and asked to display their wares more often than they would be asked again. The world honoured Canada because of Expo — probably the finest world fair ever in terms of innovation and artistic excellence. The honours were given not only for what Canadians themselves created and achieved, but because they generously allowed the entrepreneurs, artists and craftsmen from other countries artistic and creative freedom.

For the music community in Toronto, it began in '66 when Seiji Ozawa took over the Toronto Symphony from Walter Susskind. The brilliant young Japanese conductor was able to impart an imprint of greater contemporaneity — both musically and in terms of 'image' — but much of this credit lies with Susskind who nourished the orchestra along this path. Toronto was becoming one of the two or three top major cultural centres in North America — superceded by, as always, New York, and perhaps Chicago. Many of the musicians nurtured for ten years under Susskind's worldly, cosmopolitan approach were becoming instrumentalists on their own; many of them devoted their spare time towards giving solo and small chamber ensemble recitals.

Shortly after Sheila returned from Europe, three of Toronto's outstanding musicians gathered around her to form the New Piano Quartet: the TSO's principal violist, Stanley Solomon, violinist David Zafer and cellist, Donald Whitten. All of these musicians had distinguished careers back of them and it was a formidable collection indeed. Solomon was and still is, principal violist of the Toronto Symphony, a position he's held for 33 years. He has literally hundreds of broadcasts, ensemble recitals, full symphony concerts and solo concerts under his belt. Zafer, like Sheila, was a child prodigy, winning a scholarship to London's Royal College of Music at the age of nine. Arriving in Toronto in 1947, he continued to win scholarships, awards, you-name-it, until he, too, became a top symphony and solo artist. He had a considerable classical reputation but he also championed the performing of new Canadian music, and over the years he's recorded for CBC, RCA, London Records and Deutsche Grammophon. Donald Whitten's career, in 1966, included membership in the Toronto Symphony, the CBC Symphony Orchestra plus the position of lead cellist with the Promenade Symphony Orchestra. He has appeared frequently over CBC as soloist and as a member of various chamber groups; he is now the principal cellist for Ottawa's National Arts Centre Orchestra.

Music critic, Rick Kardonne, remembers chatting with Stanley Solomon on a rainy November 1979 afternoon in a restaurant near Massey Hall. "Everybody loved Sheila," Solomon told him. "We rehearsed a lot at her house. We liked her immensely; she was always so gay, witty and laughing. We all had a very nice affinity for each other, musically and as people."

David Zafer concurred, and expanded a bit. "She was really great to work with: a first-class professional. Sheila was incredibly motivated and efficient. But she had a heart of gold, you know. She was a very generous person."

The usual repertoire of the New Piano Quartet, which existed through the end of the sixties (and then, in trio form, into the early '70s) was an anthology of rather infrequently played music by Mozart, Brahms and Fauré. To supplement the repertoire a piano quintet with Harvey Siegel would sometimes be performed, along with a Fauré sonata and a Schumann A-minor sonata. Zafer admitted that with the Mozart quartet, Sheila's touch was sometimes a bit too brittle (she would try very hard to be as meticulous and precise as what she felt the music demanded); Mozart was not her real strength. But on the other pieces she shone magnificently, especially in the works of Fauré. Fauré's music was not performed a great deal at that time; he's a pre-impressionist French composer and there doesn't seem to be any valid explanation why his works were not performed more, for his dramatically soaring themes are some of the most distinctively memorable to be found anywhere in the annals of music.

The Quartet was booked through Solomon's own management agency, and they toured extensively throughout Ontario. Everywhere they went, audience response was overwhelmingly enthusiastic. They ventured into more modern music; as long as it had "free emotional soul" (Sheila's term) to it and was not merely a scientific calculation, they would boldly attempt it. And the attempts paid off. In October of 1966, the quartet played in London, Ontario and included in its program the Schumann and Fauré quartets and a piano quartet by the contemporary British composer, Anne Eggleston.

Why London, Ontario, for such an innovation? Because, in the mid-sixties, this pleasant small city of 200,000, the traditional home of Ontario true-blue Toryism, had been nurturing within its midst a small but genuinely creative urban bohemia featuring such zany innovators as artist Royden Rabinovitch and the Nihilist Spasm Band. London seemed a logical place to experiment — what we might call now an out-of-town tryout.

The audience's reaction to the concert in general was delightful — they applauded between-movement of the Fauré in much the same way as you'd get in a rock concert. According to Marion Botsford of the London *Gazette* (now defunct), the ultra-modern Eggleston quartet made the most favourable impression.

> The Schumann was intellectual, the Fauré virtuoso and the Eggleston beyond description. . . .
> The Eggleston was magnificient. Here, the New Piano Quartet was most at home . . . we saw the full potential of each musician realized in this modern psychological Piano Quartet. The group members displayed perfect rapport in exciting contemporary chamber music.
>
> (November 4, 1966)

Marion Botsford went on to describe the music in emotional terms, using words such as "yearning", "expressing anxiety", "desire", "lonely theme", and so on. She was obviously very moved by both the composition and the performance. She headlined the article. "Chamber Music Swinging" and prefaced her critique with "The New Piano Quartet has something to say". London's other daily paper, the *Free Press* (which survives today) — and the more conservative of the two — echoed the Gazette's enthusiasm, if in less emotional terms: "Performance by Toronto Ensemble Prompts Call for Second Helping".

Throughout the province they toured — Cornwall, Brockville, Kingston, Thousand Islands — all through eastern Ontario including such small towns as North Renfrew, and everywhere capacity crowds turned out to hear them, debunking the belief that the sixties was the "hip only, please" era; at the grass roots level, there is a quality of changelessness to Canada. In the heart of downtown Toronto's financial district, under the auspices of the Toronto Symphony Musicale series, the quartet performed at the new Royal Bank Building, the beginning of concerts-in-the-square amongst downtown towers which now occur as a matter of course, particularly in the summer. American tourists delight in this innovation and think Toronto a very progressive city because of it.

The Quartet was never to receive any coverage at all from the Toronto press, but despite the lack of media coverage it flourished for over four years, then was succeeded by the New Piano Trio, consisting of Sheila, David Zafer and TSO cellist (and frequent solo performer) Peter Schenkman.

Sheila's professional relationships blossomed during this period and turned out to be lasting ones. She worked with Carolyn Gundy, who began her career as a solo violinist doing concert tours throughout Ontario for the Ontario Provincial Department of Education. She, too, had been the recipient of many awards and scholarships, including the Rockefeller Foundation Scholarship in New York and a Canada Council Fellowship which took her to Europe. She was runner-up in the Carl Flesch Violin Competition and a fellow Wigmore Hall recitalist. Sheila met Carolyn at the Faculty of Music in 1952 and they first performed together publicly in 1956. Carolyn felt that even then, she knew of no one who had such diligent dedication through sheer hard work. The two women formed a lasting rapport during the '56 performance and in 1967, they performed together again, for the CBC, Brahms' *Sonata in A Major*. It was a difficult period for Carolyn for her mother was dying. It was Sheila who got Carolyn on to the program, which lifted the violinist's spirits considerably at the time.

They became very close friends from then on; perhaps Carolyn took over some of the personal territory Sheila reserved for her penpal friend, Carol (by now, Sheila was resigned to never hearing from Carol again). They had many mutual exchanges, personally and professionally — they performed Grieg's Violin-Piano Sonata in C Minor in the summer of '69 and recorded Healey Willan's violin-piano sonatas in '73 — but one that is remembered is when Sheila stepped in at the last minute, with no fee, to accompany Carolyn at a concert for the Canadian National Institute for the Blind.

"A first-rater works with first-raters; a second-rater works with third-raters," Sheila said once in response to someone's remarks about her professional generosity, particularly where friends were involved. She was immediately 'on tap' for these kinds of situations.

If the major centres in Canada were not requesting Sheila's presence on their stages, the smaller cities kept her working. There was the Grieg *Concerto in A Minor* with St. Catharines Symphony, under the direction of Milton Barnes who, during the sixties and early seventies, was music director of the Toronto Dance Theatre and the Toronto Repertory Orchestra (which he also founded), with a prolific output as a composer of some 75 works, all of which have been premiered in Canada. She repeated the Grieg concerto with the Halifax Symphony, under the direction of John Fenwick again the following March. She appeared at Stratford's summer festival of classical music series in August of 1966, then when John Fenwick called her again to ask her to pinch-hit for an artist who would not be available for their July 31st concert, Sheila quickly agreed. During the first half of the program she solo-performed five pieces by Brahms, Chopin *(Fantasia in F Minor)* and Debussy's three *Estampes* (which includes the dynamic *Evening in Granada)*. For the second half, she performed with the newly created Atlantic Orchestra (consisting of 17 musicians from the Halifax Symphony with the rest from Toronto and New York), under Fenwick's leadership, Beethoven's *Piano Concerto #1 in C Minor*. "After a tremendous ovation, she returned for an encore, performing the haunting and delicate Chopin *Mazurka in A Minor* (Marcia Loynd, "Audience Impressed with Pianist's Concert",*Guardian,* Charlottetown, Monday, August 1, 1966).

The following year there was a concert in Peterborough, one at the Memorial University of Newfoundland (for a CBC Centennial concert), then to Guelph where she teamed up with fellow Torontonian, piano accompanist Leo Barkin. Sheila was playing in her own country, as she wanted to, but she had yet to perform in Vancouver, Winnipeg — which she dearly wanted to do — or Montreal. Wherever she performed, she treated every concert with the same degree of preparation and respect as she had treated her concerts in Vienna and London.

"A performance is a performance and it doesn't matter where it is. I prepare for every concert in exactly the same way, working no harder for any particular engagement over another. I want to give the best performance I can give, whether it's Wigmore Hall in London or here, tomorrow night," she explained to Libby McKean of the Halifax *Mail-Star* (March 9, 1966).

Ever since the Houston concert and her European tour, Sheila had occasionally kept a diary of sorts — not day by day, but for either important events or simply when the spirit moved her. Sometimes they were just thoughts and observations written on scraps of paper, saved perhaps to be recopied into a letter to someone. In conversation, Sheila's nervous energy and natural wit invariably took over her personna and the introspective thoughtfulness of her personality got lost in the excitement of the moment. She talked like she performed, with great emotional intensity and intelligent vitality. Writing was her one way of communicating the quieter, "inner" Sheila, whether to friends via the mails, or simply to herself. She was particularly prone to writing on airplanes, her emotional eneregy drained by the past performance, her reasoning intellect sharpened. On the flight back from Charlottetown (dated August 2, 1966) en route to the Stratford summer music festival, she wrote herself a little 'essay'.

SHEILA — JUST THINKING
ON BEING A CONCERT ARTIST:

I really do appreciate the favorable reviews I have been getting for many years. However, to me it becomes repetitious. The once highly important reviews that meant so much to me no longer matter. I would, rather, like to somewhat familiarize the public with what it's like to be an artist.

What are the feelings of an artist before an important concert? What are the aims of performers? And, most of all, why are they pursuing an art with such intensity? Is it for materialistic gains? Not really. There is something more beyond that.

"Please listen to my music" — or — "Watch me skate". "I'll pay you if necessary. But hear me. Watch me. I wish to perform for you." The most important essence in the life of a performer is to perform. An artist lives mainly for the excitement that prevails in performing, and the overwhelming satisfaction of knowing that you are providing enjoyment to an audience created through your talent and your dedication to music. If you combine all the qualifications an artist must possess, you might derive some measure of success. One must, however, remember that there are sacrifices to be made and a price to be paid along the long, bumpy, frustrating road.

STAGE FRIGHT

Whether they call it butterflies, paralyzing fear, or exciting anticipation, you must project confidence when you come onto the stage. Confidence is highly contagious. It grips and holds the attention of the audience, and lingers in the mind long after the concert is over, whereas a poor performance is forgotten by the time they reach the exit door.

The only point on which all the artists agree is — whatever you choose to call it, anticipation, energy, nervous tension — stage fright in the nicest sense of the word is an absolutely necessary prelude to a good performance. I really feel that an artist must be charged up with nervous energy in order to reach the emotional depths of his performance, which occurs prior to the moment one steps out from behind the magic curtain and onto the stage.

For me, the stage is like a cathedral. Says Louis Quillico: "I respect the stage. I say a little prayer before the performance, because I am a coward. Thank you, God, you have given me a talent, so please help me. And you'll be surprised at how much help you get."

We put ourselves through torture, not for the applause or because of self-interest, but because we need to give, and we are afraid our gift won't be well received. We are lucky people. We have the opportunity for incredible self-expression and with that comes the responsibility of helping other people to discover themselves. Humility, grace, sensitivity and humour are tied together in order to perform well. The more polished your performance, the more nervous you'll be, because then you sense everything; you can hear things that nobody else hears. So you expect more of yourself. I did a concert in Brantford, Ontario, a half-hour later than scheduled because I flew in from New York and the plane was late. I got out of the airport, tumbled into a waiting car, and drove at neck-breaking speed to get there. I hadn't eaten all day and was on the verge of collapse. In spite of it all, the critics and the audience were ecstatic with my performance. No matter how I played that evening, I would have been great, because it was all due to circumstances that the concert was a tremendous success.

CRITICS

Alexander Brott, as a conductor, has an interesting view of critics. "I really believe that critics aren't talking to me at all. Criticism is a profession in its own right; the critic performs for his own audience, the newspaper readers."

Lately, I have been thinking about artists in general, competitions, performances, and recording sessions; thoughts which I shall endeavour to explore and perhaps shed some light on those sensitive subjects which are not familiar to the general public. I wish that the words which I'm about to write could talk. They would, in simple terminology, expand and overflow into a book that would explain and express some of the anxieties, frustrations, and even fright that keep on haunting performers in all areas of entertainment. Above all, these words should tell the music critics what one experiences in playing classical music, knowing that they, the critics, are there. I, myself, am always prepared to do a concert at one hour's notice. I practice many hours every single day, and have many scores at my fingertips. The only thing one can't prepare for is the emotional excitement and the flood of energy that pervades one's soul, which is the prelude to a performance that increases in intensity until it explodes through your fingers on the keyboard. When that happens, the world ceases to exist, and everything is blotted out of your mind until the concert is over.

Many competitions and performances are indelibly carved into my mind. Although I won most of the competitions, and received rave reviews through the years, the pressure has nevertheless always been the same. You are sitting, waiting for your name to be called. You are listening to other competitors playing behind closed doors. Your name will soon be called. You still have ample time to think, and you are emotionally prepared to play as well as you know you can. However, the more time you have to think, the more you realize that you are losing your power of concentration, and you begin to doubt your capabilities. Everyone seems to be playing better than you, and the palms of your hands are getting wet. Similar feelings exist before a concert, although the situation is quite different. You are not worried about your competitors, but you are nevertheless aware of the yet unseen audience that has come to enjoy a good performance. You also know that music critics are waiting for you with their sharp pencils in hand. You are nervously pacing the floor behind the stage curtain, where the silence is drowned out in the unbearable noise coming from the audience in the concert hall. The lights are finally dimmed, and the curtain slowly starts rising. You take a deep breath and walk onto the stage. You proceed towards the huge piano that is silently waiting for you, and you are thinking; "I hope that the gown I am wearing (or the jacket, whichever the case may be) will not restrict the movements of my arms." Suddenly the stage lights are glaring into your eyes, and everything transforms into glitter and glamour. The deafening applause empties the pockets of your mind. You are only vaguely aware of the thunderous ovation that's coming from hundreds of hands.

You sit down daintily, carefully, whatever. Your fingers begin to challenge the keyboard. One finger trips over a note of a difficult phrase, but you don't know why. Yesterday, and the day before, it was easy. You start spinning a single thread and weave it into an intricate sonata. Emotions take over. You begin to feel that your spirit is rising. Your confidence is slowly returning, and you start to make the piano do what you want it to do. You dig gently, but deeply, into the keys and draw beautiful music from every note. Or, you make your fingers fly lightning fast up and down the keyboard. You are hearing the pure crystal brilliance of fast passages, and you are lost in a world unknown to anyone but yourself. At this precise moment your life-span only lasts as long as the concert. Your mind's eye becomes a vacuum: oblivious to everything around you. You can't permit yourself to visualize your score; if you do, you'll get lost in a sea of pages and pages of music. Your emotions are charged up, and you are reaching out to weave melodies and make the piano sing. You are trying to draw every drop of beautiful tones out of the instrument. You can feel the vibrations in the tips of your fingers. You are speaking a universal language that is easy and enjoyable to understand. You communicate with people through your music. The response is overwhelming. The audience finds it impossible to hold back their sense of appreciation, and spontaneous applause bursts out during the performance. The concert is over, but they want more; and after several encores and explosive applause, you disappear behind the curtain while the ovation continues. You are exhausted but happy; you know that they appreciated and understood.

The more an artist performs, the more he realizes that his profession is the main force that keeps him living. If you performed well, you are a star. If, on the other hand, you had an off-night, as it sometimes happens, you are mediocre, in spite of the rave reviews you have accumulated over many years. They are all forgotten in one bad performance. "You are as good as your last performance." I therefore make every possible effort to feel relaxed before I appear on stage. I try to blot the whole world out of my mind, and to concentrate with full confidence on the music score. I calm down and become a performer. That's the sweetest time of my life. I willingly surrender to the music, and get carried away into oblivion. I expose my heart and soul to the *creativity and emotions that I feel, and willingly yield myself to the audience, gathering strength from their enthusiasm.*

The concert is over, but the applause is still ringing in my ears. I'm pleased with the results. The hall is empty, and the orchestra has left. Only I and some friends and fans are still in my dressing-room. They are waiting for my autograph, but I'm still in a sort of daze.

By the time I get home around 2 a.m., I try to unwind but find it impossible. I toss and turn until morning. My husband Bill brings in the morning newspaper. I quickly read the reviews. I read them thirstily, only to be amazed that the critics are not in agreement in some areas. One criticizes the very same part of the program that another one praises. It makes me think they are not reviewing the same concert, but why speculate? It's only their opinion. They apparently didn't understand me. How, then, could they understand my music?

This, then, is a brief account by an artist: how a concert pianist lives and feels, before, during and after a performance. It's a difficult life, but I love it. There is nothing in the world that could contribute to my life more than being an artist, excluding my family, of course.

After a heavy, demanding concert, I don't go near the piano for several days. I am drained emotionally, and fatigue numbs every muscle. My concentration has to be recharged. After a few restless days and sleepless nights, I gradually begin to feel guilty for not practising; and slowly, sort of lazily, I begin to work again in order to keep my fingers in shape. However, a letter, a telegram or a phone call can suddenly change it all and I have to start preparing a new program for another concert. I start working six to eight hours a day. My energy begins charging up again. And I get lost in practising for the upcoming concert.

In December of 1967 Sheila did a broadcast for the CBC and played, among other compositions, the *Capriccio* by Felix Mendelssohn, giving a truly brilliant performance. Letters poured in to Sheila congratulating her. Murray Adaskin, Professor of Music at the University of Saskatchewan in Saskatoon, is only an example of the professionals who had heard, and commented on, that particular performance.

Dear Sheila,

What a perfectly wonderful broadcast over the CBC in your recent performance! You played the Capriccio beautifully — I couldn't wish for a lovelier performance. Aside from your superb mastery, I felt that your interpretation was intelligently clear, sensitive and warm, in fact you seemed to play the work with that rare ingredient — 'loving care'.

In any case, I want you to know how very pleased and delighted I was to hear such a beautiful performance and to tell you how deeply grateful I am to you.

Much, much success and my fondest good wishes.

Yours,
(signed) Murray Adaskin

January 3, 1968.

One rare delight followed another. Sheila and Bill adopted another child, a boy this time, Derek. Sheila seemed to have reached a peak of happiness — in her daily journal, the kind with large spaces for each of the days, for her days were very full at this time, she wrote — *I have a darling little boy. He is adorable and I love him very much. When I look at his round pink face, blue eyes and a wisp of blond hair, I feel as if my heart is bursting with pride. I consider myself fortunate to have such a beautiful family, plus a satisfying career, and I thank God every day for His kindness.*

Mr. Henig recalls this time very well — first of all, Sheila, absorbed in the new baby was home more, and father and daughter saw more of each other. "She felt she was a full-fledged mother now and that seemed to be so very important to her — that she be a success as a mother and as an artist. It was a special time for her — everything in her life was working like clockwork, which sometimes happens in a person's life, absolutely everything comes together and you get such a wonderful sense of peace and fulfillment. This was Sheila at this time. She was never as happy again."

By this time Sheila and Bill had moved to their final home in the beautiful Bayview area. She took great care in choosing the interior decor, utilizing the same sensitivities of elegance and innovation which characterized her performances and her taste in fashion. Her home was not a showplace but a beautifully livable home. Her love of animals was now almost legendary, and the family pet menagerie had grown. Sheila sang in the choir and, as she had said on more than one occasion, she felt singing was still her first love; here she performed as much for her own enjoyment as anybody else's; there did not seem to be the need to be absolutely perfect, or at least the need to strive for the absolute. "I'm in love with classical music," she remarked to her father. "It talks to me through a kind of intellectual passion, voice or piano. Both are equally important and can bring one closer to infinity."

Mr. Henig noticed that as she moved into the last decade of her life, Sheila became more philosophical — he worried because he felt perhaps there was something bothering her which she couldn't define, because to all intents and purposes, she was very, very happy at this time. Although she was ecstatic over the new baby, he felt that perhaps this event served to draw the dichotomies of her life into sharper focus — "I can't remain detached from classical music," she told her father at the time, when he inquired whether she would take a 'sabbatical' from performing. "My family, my home, they're very dear and important to me, but music controls my life, it's at the very centre of everything I do. I have to be deeply involved in it in order to enjoy living."

PART IV
The Professional Milieu

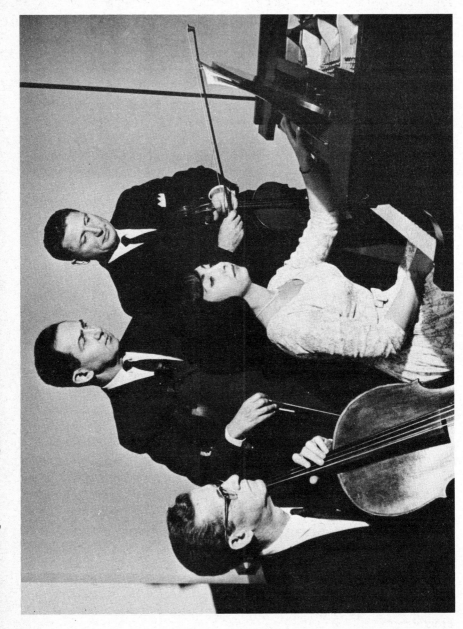

The New Piano Quartet: left to right, Donald Whitten, David Zafer, Stanley Solomon, and Sheila.

The Professional Milieu

On December 28, 1968, the flower-child dewy-eyed hope for a better future era died at Altamont racetrack, a mass, free, Rolling Stones rock concert deteriorated into a bloody riot in which people were killed. The end of the '60s brought, as it turned out, an apparent end to the counterculture. The youth nurtured in the '60s — and consequently, the entire pop culture scene which had become so dependent on the youth attitudes of the baby-boom generation — abandoned hope in the future, withdrew into themselves and nostalgically looked back into the past. "Altamont changed a lot of people's heads" seemed to be the slogan of the documentary movie of that event, *Gimme Shelter.* Newly into the '80s, it will be a while before we can, culturally, sort out the influence of the seventies — if there was much of an influence — and give it a nametag for posterity. "Let it Be" seemed to take over for the 'making it be' energy of the '60s; the nostalgic flashback to the '50s, "Grease", seemed to have replaced the delightful hopefulness of "Hair" — and it wouldn't be until the mid to late 70s that anything of a definable nature replaced the high-profile music of the hippie-yippie years, when punk and new wave began to appear. The '70s were always on the brink of a total change back to the reactionary, but this too eluded the decade as some of the old 'enlightenment' seemed to linger around, waiting for resurgence. There are many who say that the reactionary has finally dug its heels in, as the first year of the '80s ends, but it is too soon to tell.

Whatever the new cultural climate would be in the '70s, Sheila's life was now a continual pursuit of concert work. She had established herself as a world-class professional and gathered about her colleagues of like mind and abilities. Her life was very much a solidifying of past experience and a solid projection into creating a work environment — particularly in terms of the people she worked with — which would nourish her into middle age. If she was dissatisfied with critics' response, or the kind of concert work available to her — rather than the number of concerts — she had a peer group to which she belonged and could commiserate with, for they shared much the same experience in the effort to become involved in quality work in their profession.

Throughout the early '70s there was a great deal of talk about "preserving a Canadian culture", so much so that legislation was passed to impose Canadian content quotas on the broadcast media, which seemed to impose restrictions on American and European imports but did nothing to raise the level of production of popular entertainment. The general mass of Canadians still wanted what their American counterparts were getting only they had to suffice with Canadian imitations of it rather than the original. Indigenous creative artists, such as the Canadian serious music composers, didn't seem to be getting any more benefits from the new 'Canada-first' quotas than they had before they were installed. They may have received more notice in the press and broadcast media, but they were not becoming any more influential either amongst Canadians at large, or internationally.

Sheila, probably realizing that her own future as a mature artist would be affected by the kind of promotion her colleagues received — and also from a genuine interest in new music that was good — would align herself as an artist with as many Canadian composers as she could.

The number of small performing groups based in Toronto were growing. Sheila's New Piano Quartet — now a trio — was going strong; Walter Babiak's New Chamber Orchestra (originally Canadian Chamber Orchestra, founded by Babiak in 1969) was producing a yearly season. The conductorship of the TSO would change again, Ozawa would leave and Karel Ancerl would take over until his death, to be replaced by Andrew Davis from England. The Toronto Repertory Orchestra, founded by Milton Barnes in the '60s, just made it into the '70s and then floundered. There was a lot of ensemble work happening in and around Toronto, and at least some of the repertoire was Canadian composed. In the mid-70s Camerata was founded and not only did they play wonderful music, but they added a hitherto unknown element for a Canadian serious music ensemble — they knew how to tack an element of showbiz onto their act. Mid-to-late '70s, the Canadian Brass took off and actually became popular and were 'in demand' in their own country.

So there was a wide spectrum which ranged across the old question of how does a Canadian artist survive in their own country. What appeared to be evident was that they fared better if they attached themselves to an ensemble and made the ensemble the 'star'; individually, the Canadian artist — composer, sculptor, musician, actor, dancer — was knocking his or her head against brick walls. A generalization, perhaps, but worth taking an analytical note of it.

Professionally, in Sheila's terms, her next important concert was at the National Gallery of Art in Washington, D.C. (1971). Her programming was all-important now, and she chose a very demanding one for this concert. For the first half there was Brahms and Liszt — Brahms *G-Minor Ballade,* the *E Flat Minor Intermezzo* and the *C Major Intermezzo,* plus the difficult Liszt *B-Minor Sonata.* For the second half of the program she chose works by two Canadians — Oskar Morawetz and Srul Irving Glick. The concert itself was a success, but that will come later. What was quite extraordinary was that Sheila was using this opportunity — a major performance in the U.S. — to promote music by Canadian composers. She was not self-effacing enough to do this simply to help old friends or for the good of fellow countrymen. She performed these compositions because, as an artist, a pianist, they were exciting, challenging works for her and they gave her the same kind of satisfaction, as a performer, as the 'old masters'.

Both these composers hailed from her student days. Morawetz had been her primary professor while she was a student at the Faculty of Music; Srul Glick went back even further for they had been in high school together and had shared the stage in Gilbert & Sullivan productions. Morawetz belonged to that generation of composers who had come to Toronto between 1900 and 1950, who found the city a pleasant, even placid, home ground in which to create while being readily accessible to the major centres of New York, London and Paris. Morawetz was born in Czechoslovakia in 1917 and left in December 1938, shortly before the Nazi conquest. He moved to Canada in 1940. His orchestra works have been performed by nearly 150 orchestras in Europe, the Americas, Australia and Asia. In Toronto he earned a doctorate in music from the University of Toronto, but in composition he taught himself. Over the years he is perhaps best known for his compositions, *Diary of Anne Frank, Passacaglia to the Memory of Kennedy* and his *Memorial to Martin Luther King,* probably because these works are what the media would call 'high profile pieces'. But it was his *Scherzo* for solo piano which Sheila loved and played frequently in recitals and concerts. The *Scherzo* was originally performed by the same Rudolf Firkusny who resurrected Dvorak's piano concerto, another of Sheila's favourites; it was composed in 1947 when Morawetz was a young successful concert pianist and the piece was meant to be a popular tour-de-force especially suitable for the dramatic temperament of an interpreter such as Sheila. Wherever she performed it, the *Scherzo* would receive acclaim. Rick Kardonne, Toronto music critic, speaks of Morawetz' music as having influences of Prokofieff and Hindemith. But he claims that the way Morawetz fused them all together and then created his own innovations is what imprints his works with a style uniquely his own. Morawetz' works first came into prominence after winning the Canadian Composers and Authors Association (CAPAC) award in 1944 and '45; many other honours of international importance followed. Some of his shorter works have become standard repertoire with many orchestras the world over, including the *Carnival Overture* (introduced in Toronto by guest-conductor Sir Adrian Boult and premiered in the U.S. by Rafael Kubelik with the Chicago Symphony); *Overture to a Fairy Tale* (premiered at Stratford Music Festival, 1956); and *Divertimento for Strings,* which was chosen to represent Canadian music at the Brussels World's Fair in 1958. However, as mentioned, he remains best known for his three memorial works to John F. Kennedy, Martin Luther King and Anne Frank — "An interesting comment, in a way, on the spirit of the man who wrote them, for they were composed in honour of three towering essences of the human spirit, all of whom were cut down before their positive influence on humanity as a whole were to be fully realized." (Rick Kardonne)

As an interesting sidenote, Otto Frank gave Morawetz a gift after the Premiere of *The Diary of Anne Frank,* a small silver dish received by him and his wife as a wedding gift in 1925.

"It was the most moving gift imaginable," remarked Morawetz at the time. "When I think of how little must remain of his earlier life, I am incredibly grateful for his generosity."

Morawetz was very, very fond of Sheila — both as a person and as a

Oskar Morawetz and Golda Meir at a special performance at Temple Beth Tzedec, with Sheila and many other musicians taking part.

musician. He had taught her and helped to form her eventual essence as a solo performer. "She was wonderful to work with," he said, "a terrific sightreader." He was deeply grateful for her choice of the Scherzo at so many of her important concerts.

Although Srul Glick's relationship with Sheila dated back to high school, his major influence and help came from his position as serious music producer of shows and records for CBC. They collaborated many times in an almost ideal professional relationship between solo performer-interpreter and a producer who was a composer in his own right. For the Washington, D.C. concert she performed his *Four Preludes for Piano*.

It was a particularly important concert because many a career has been launched in that city; the presence of Paul Hume of the Washington Post (considered one of the two top critics in North America) made this equal in importance to a New York debut, Sheila remarked in a diary account of the recital. *My Houston concert had been so long before that I felt that I had to prove myself all over again to the American public and critics.*

I chose a very demanding program and, needless to say, was extremely nervous on the day of the concert. When I went to rehearse in the morning I found, to my horror, that the concert was to take place in a large marble "garden" setting — not a hall at all and since there was nobody in the "garden" at that time, the echo was unbelievable. I was practically in tears but the gentleman in charge, Richard Bales, assured me that with an audience everything would be fine. And so it was. No echo.

I was fortunate to have had a large, enthusiastic audience. One young man came backstage after the concert and said that it had inspired him to write a poem (in French) during the concert. He said that he would send me a copy but I never received it (a pity).

I was very upset that day when I was told that the critic, Paul Hume, was not going to be present (his review was really the raison d'être of the whole concert) because he no longer came to these concerts but sent someone else. I was disappointed but also somewhat more relaxed knowing he was not going to be there. Imagine my amazement to open the morning paper the next day and see a review by him and what a wonderful review. She tacked a copy of the review to the diary page.

IMPRESSIVE LISZT

Sheila Henig moved from a strong opening in Brahms to an all-over impressive delivery of the Liszt Sonata last night in her National Gallery concert. The young Canadian pianist has all the deep-fingered control to make late Brahms sing and ring. She played the G Minor Ballade, the E Flat Minor Intermezzo and the ineffably gracious C Major Intermezzo from the composor's late years and gave each its proper mellow message. The long buildup that is the glory of the piece in E Flat Minor was one of the fine achievements.

The secret of the Liszt Sonata lies in the way it is made to hang together. How not to rush without undue lingering, how to apportion delicacy without undue stress on unimportant notes, and where and how to deliver the thunder that is one of the sonata's grand messages.

Miss Henig is impressive in her total management of the mountainous work. Best in its largest statements, she rushed a bit early in the music, fussed here and there in its lyrical passages. But her fugue was superb, and the greatest musical moments brought out her finest playing.

After the intermission, she paid tribute to her fellow Canadian composers, Srul Glick and Oskar Morawetz before ending the evening with a brilliant performance of the Second Sonata by Prokofieff.

The Morawetz Scherzo is an unusually effective piece of writing, both for the instrument and its generous originality.

Miss Henig had no trouble in capturing each capricious mood of the Prokofieff Sonata, while the technique that carried her easily through Liszt was more than sufficient for one of his descendents.

— Paul Hume
Washington Post (Summer 1971)

Sheila continued in her diary — *Mr. Bales said it was one of the best reviews he* [Paul Hume] *had given* anyone *performing in Washington in a long time.*

The reason Paul Hume had come, apparently, was due to a mutual friend. A man who had heard me play in Halifax some years before had called Mr. Hume and told him to be sure to come to my concert — which he did. Talk about luck!

I was sure that that review would open many doors; but although I got some publicity when I returned home, I feel that I have yet to be fully appreciated in my home country. However, I'm not sure that the exhausting and lonely life of a touring artist is for me, anyway.

Sheila gave another spectacular performance with the New Chamber Orchestra at the Hart House Great Hall (University of Toronto). Walter Babiak guest-conducted two runaway virtuoso works, Shostakovich's *Piano Concerto #2 for String Orchestra and Trumpet* (the trumpeter being Bill Phillips) and Ernest Bloch's *Concerto Grosso* for string orchestra and piano. Both these works are innovative, extremely demanding — for all the instruments — and to be performed successfully, asks for the maximum output of emotional energy and technique from the solo performers.

Babiak, who had worked with many a fine musician, was, if anything, a little awed by Sheila's performance. "Everything Sheila did was crystal clear. She was able to sort and draw out all of the inner subtleties of a composition, no matter how complex," he remarked. "She was always most akin to the real intentions of the composer. And yet she was such a good ensemble player. She had no 'follow' syndrome. Never did she have to stop and ask the conductor, 'What are you doing here?'"

Healey Willan is a sort of Canadian controversy; he seems to epitomize Canada's earlier cultural colonialism. A quote from the program note of an album cover, Sheila performing Healey Willan's *Concerto for Piano in C Minor*, speaks of him thusly: "The spirit (of his music) is one of Victorian comfort, without anguished spiritual struggle or suggestions of over-ripeness or decadence. It is a momento of a Canada now dead, with a small academic colonial culture and a certain innocence; the result of our insulation from the tension afflicting the cultural centres, which lapped on our shores only as faint waves." This could be described as a typical early seventies description of Willan — but he is also the acknowledged "father of Canadian music", whose prolific 88-year-life produced an impressive array of original compositions which knowledgeably incorporated and fused every European musical style in existence from baroque to late romantic — as long as they appeared prior to the turn of the present century. Today it is fashionable in trendy Canadian cultural-nationalist circles to deride Healey Willan as being hopelessly old fashioned and totally ignorant of Canadian indigenous musical roots and trends. It is true his compositional development terminated sometime before Debussy, but nobody can deny the first-rate degree of musical scholarship and excellence which he imprinted upon grass-roots Canadiana during the several decades when he ruled supreme. He was born in Balham, England, in 1880 and came to Canada in 1913 to take up the position of head of the theory department of the Toronto Conservatory of Music. He was also appointed organist and choirmaster of St. Paul's Church on Bloor Street and from these two positions in the music world, he began his prodigous output, making an important contribution to church music which is readily acknowledged throughout the English-speaking world.

Healey Willan's work as a kindly guide to his many students encouraged composers and performers of ensuing generations. When Sheila first approached him and indicated to him her desire to learn his *Concerto in C Minor for Piano and Orchestra*, he was most obliging and he did everything possible to help her despite his advanced age at the time (he was 85). This was in the '60s and she performed the concerto for the first time in 1965 for a CBC-Toronto Symphony broadcast, which was one of Sir Ernest's last appearances as guest conductor of the orchestra after Walter Susskind took it over. This event would apparently have little to do with Sheila's life in the '70s except that it was a superb performance which caught the attention of musically influential people, and in 1972 she was invited by her old friend, Srul Glick, to record the Concerto with the CBC Vancouver Chamber Orchestra and to give a live performance before the recording session with Mario Bernardi and the National Arts Centre Orchestra.

The National Arts Centre had been born out of Canada's Centennial year (1967) fervour and it was to be the core of a concept which would transform Ottawa from a pretty but sleepy backwater into a shining landmark on the international cultural circuit and to be, above all, a showplace for Canadian culture and talent. The Orchestra, and its conductor Bernardi, have lived up to its mandate and have become over the years a much-loved, much acclaimed musical institution.

On the eve of the concert (April 30, 1972) Sheila told the Ottawa *Citizen* "I'm really one of the only people who plays Willan these days. I was so pleased when Mario Bernardi suggested it. I feel that it is a major romantic piano concerto which has been unduly neglected." As it turned out, Bernardi did not conduct the work, for he had been called to Pittsburgh to guest-conduct in an emergency and Victor Feldbrill of the Toronto Symphony ended up directing this event. "She (Sheila) was very dedicated to the work . . . She very much wanted to perform it," remarked Feldbrill.

The *Citizen's* Lauretta Thistle had mixed feelings about the work, although not about Sheila's performance. She described the Concerto as being a "strongly lyrical work thoroughly in the romantic tradition of Tchaikovsky and Grieg, with some Rachmaninoffian flourishes in the brass and strings. It abounds in melody, and much of the denser scoring has interesting texture. The solo part asks for persuasive playing and considerable technical brilliance. These Miss Henig was able to supply." Then she described the Concerto as being "far from representative of this century". She scored it as being "conservative and tentative, and its experiments were neither very daring nor very engrossing — the sum is not really much more than a work of historical interest".

However, it was a good warmup for Sheila's recording session in Vancouver, and it was on the flight out west where she wrote down the short passage which opens this book.

One wonders if perhaps Sheila wasn't wasting her time concentrating on works of this kind, possibly hurting her image in the music circles which seem to have such influence on who plays what, when, by dedicating herself to a composer who was not in favour. Like a lot of the early 20th century Canadian music, Willan was an educational 'tool'; such major composers of today's Canadian scene as Oscar-nominee Louis Applebaum, who have created genuinely original works, have benefited greatly under Willan's tutelage and in the nature of these things, there will probably be, at some time, a resurgence of interest in his work for historical reasons.

All through 1972 and 1973, Sheila and Srul Glick were hard at work making records for the CBC, with Glick, meanwhile, composing his own compositions which would be performed and premiered fairly regularly all through the '70s. Back in '63, Srul was recording the Toronto Symphony at Toronto's Hallmark Studios for a radio broadcast. Some extra money had been made available from the CBC and he phoned Sheila — "Could you record a disc within three days?" She replied, "I'll do it". And she did. As Srul remembers — probably in reference to this particular event — she was a tremendously hard worker and an extremely fast learner. Among her rare, unique capacities was her ability to listen to a "take" which either she had done previously, or that someone else had done, get a new musical interpretative idea of her own and then do it her own way — perfectly. Srul was tremendously impressed with this ability, particularly back in '63 when she was considered, if not 'up-and-coming', still a young pianist without a mountain of experience behind her.

Sheila and the entire Glick family — which is large, clever and talented, whose members include doctors, film investors and gifted musicians — were very close friends. Sheila had a very special friendship with Srul's wife, Dorothy Sandler-Glick, also a fine concert pianist. They would often gather in the sturdy Victorian house which was Srul's home for musicales, reminiscent of Srul's student days perhaps, when he studied in Paris with Darius Milhaud. At any rate, it would be a rare enclave of talent under one roof, informally gathered to "play music". Sheila and Srul often talked about various interpretations of the music they were in the midst of recording on their working days.

Glick produced several CBC records during this period (early '70s) with Sheila; the finest was undoubtedly *Music of Pianist-Composers*, beginning with Morawetz' *Scherzo,* and continuing with Prokofieff's *Piano Sonata #2 in D Minor,* which had been such a big hit during Sheila's tour of Europe. The second side of the album comprised one of Sheila's specialities, Franz Liszt, beginning with his *Grand Concert Etude #2,* characterized by its subdued grandeur and followed by the gay, frothy *Les Jeux d'Eaux a la Villa de l'Este,* which is an interesting progenitor to the delicate Debussy impressionistic moods. The album concludes with Liszt's *Les Funerailles,* which is one of his most famous "grand" themes. Sheila's approach avoided the temptation of bombasity for a more thoughtful one, allowing the sombre undertones to be more concentrated.

Srul was constantly researching the Canadian cultural heritage and his influence on Sheila at this time was probably much more than simply someone who got her work. He opened further doors for her own perceptions of Canadian 'culture', where she fitted in, if she did, and how. Always, there were pockets of feverish activity, a lot of exciting work to be done, and then nothing. Sheila was reaching the crux of a dilemma — multi-faceted and unquestionably painful and difficult for there was no solution. She, like every blessed Canadian artist and performer, was having to face, square-on, the problem of how she was going to continue her life's work in a country which had an abundance of gifted people but did not have either the population to support them in a fulfilling enough way, or did not have the inclination to do so. It could be a mixture of both — simple logistics point to the probable presence of the first — or the singular blame could be placed on the second: no one seems to have figured it out yet, although the dilemma, and the endless round of the question, "why?", reappears with alarming frequency to this day.

Pre-concert interviews were now stressing her domestic scene as much as her professional responsibilities. This would be the early seventies —1972-73

— when 'career' women were tackling similar problems the world over; International Women's Year was only two years away. Both the *Toronto Star*, and the Ottawa *Citizen*, preluded her performance with the NAC orchestra with the fact that here was, basically, a "working mother". "FAMILY COMES FIRST WITH PIANIST" said the *Star's* Lotta Dempsey. "When I went to visit the artist and her family at their new home in Willowdale," wrote Miss Dempsey, "Mrs. Sidney had just finished decorating.

> "Ask me when I did the Healey Willan Concerto in C Minor with the CBC Symphony (a taping session six years ago) and I'll tell you it was when Shawna was just a few weeks old. It's a tremendous but very demanding work, and I had five weeks to learn it, with the singular opportunity to confer with the composer (now deceased) and to know how happy he was with the performance.
> "As you know, Liszt's Concerto No. 1 in E Flat Major is also a composition which requires the best of an artist.
> "When we taped that for the CBC-TV series Music To See (aired last Sunday) Derek had chicken-pox and I got three hours sleep the night before."
> So the artist-cum-mother has the same problems as the professional woman, factory worker or steno with two roles to play.
> Like most of the rest of us, Sheila Henig wouldn't have it any other way.
> Her home is very important, and she is able to keep a weather eye on the children while practicing up to five hours a day, seven days a week.
>
> (July 16, 1961)

Lotta Dempsey went on to detail the new decorating schemes Sheila and Bill had begun in their home.

Vivian Macdonald of the Ottawa *Citizen,* concentrated on much the same elements, beginning the article with a low-key 'ordinary guy' touch —"Sheila Henig describes herself as a frustrated singer and a frustrated dancer. In reality, she is an accomplished concert pianist." She, too, mentioned Sheila's practicing schedule, but here Sheila was quoted as saying, "Unfortunately it is not sound-proofed but it does help muffle the roar of the children about the house" — a far cry from her student days when the family had to live in the basement.

Sheila's public personna seemed quite at odds with her private dilemma; she appeared to be a vivacious, 'laid-back' mom who took the double role of artist-mother with rueful good nature. She remarked to Vivian Macdonald that although neither of her children were taking piano lessons — "Children that young do not really concentrate" — Shawna was taking Saturday ballet lessons at the National Ballet School and both children were models, appearing regularly in television commercials. Many of Sheila's colleagues and friends said she had a natural 'gift' for self-effacement, and so it would appear as Miss Macdonald finished her article.

Sheila and her family: Bill, Derek (on her lap) and Shawna, standing.

With practicing, teaching, chauffering her young models and running a training school for domestics (she's had 25 housekeepers in seven years), there isn't much time for attending concerts.

When she does attend a concert she prefers it to be a vocal performance. "One can become saturated with the sound of the piano," she explained. "And after all, I am a frustrated singer."

She holds degrees in both singing and piano but at the age of 18 chose to concentrate on piano because "my voice just wasn't good enough". She does her singing now in the choir of Toronto's Temple Emanu-El, often as a soloist on High Holidays.

Her repertoire as a pianist is strictly classical. "I enjoy other kinds of music but play only classical. I envy people like Peter Nero who have a gift for improvising but I have no talent for it."

Her favourite composers are Brahms and Chopin. "I'm not terribly avant garde. I don't do 12-tone works because I'm really not sympathetic to that kind of music. I don't dig it."

April 20, 1972

Again, prior to the same NAC concert featuring the Willan Concerto, Ottawa reporter Eunice Gardiner stressed the domestic problems and added another dimension to Sheila.

> Sheila Henig, the Toronto pianist acclaimed for her work at the keyboard both here and abroad, is a woman not just of many talents, but of many interests.
>
> "This is my year for writing letters to the editors," she laughed.
>
> With two small children, Derek in nursery school and Shawna, almost seven, at day school, Miss Henig and her husband, pharmacist William Sidney, are perturbed by the lack of protection for children in buses.

Sheila had, evidently, written letters concerning the problem, which promptly snowballed until she and her immediate community were involved in getting provincial support for better school buses. Like other interviewers, she mentioned that Sheila had given up concert tours until her children were more independent.

> She wants to perform as often as possible and will continue to teach a half dozen advanced piano students.

A couple of paragraphs on the Willan piece with a quote or two about how Sheila felt about performing the work, a mention that she was going to give a performance in Sarnia as part of the Community Concerts program plus the fact that Sheila and Bill were members of an amateur drama workshop group, followed.

Petite, but fiery, the pianist shrugs when asked, "and how can you manage a family, a big house and your music?"

"You can just say that I live on Vitamin E. And I've had the help of 25 housekeepers," she added, more than a little ruefully.

In reality, Sheila's perception of her life was considerably more than what appeared on the women's pages. She was forever writing down insights — into herself or music — on bits of paper, dating them and then stuffing them into drawers, perhaps with the idea of some day putting them together as a kind of 'retrospective' on herself, although to anybody's knowledge she never had any aspiration to have an auto-biography published. Dated March 15th, 1973, she wrote a worried note to herself, about getting good reviews —*I confess that it's very satisfying, but also frightening. One reviewer summed up my whole life — that is, all the nice things reviewers have said about me — into one package! I only hope that I can live up to it; I would be terribly embarrassed if I got a bad review now, I am forever hoping that it won't happen. When I do a concert I am always left with a feeling that I could have done better. The critics apparently don't share my view.*

She was fortunate, she once remarked, that she had met a number of interesting and famous people during her career, "strangely enough, mainly right here in Toronto".

In '73 she was extremely excited about working with Arthur Fiedler, who was to conduct her performance with the Toronto Symphony at Ontario Place, a lakefront performance forum which programmed different major entertainment personalities all summer long at probably the lowest admission price in the world, $1.00 — in inflation-plagued 1981 it's $3.50, still a bargain! She was filled with apprehension for she was playing a new concerto for the first time, and, of course, there was 'The Maestro'.

He barked at me the first time I slipped on a note (which is frightening and humiliating). We couldn't agree on a proper tempo for the ending (he took it all much too fast) and I left that rehearsal not even wanting to return the next day. The piano was also not to my liking and I managed to rip the skin off a few cuticles trying a glissando (I did it again the next day — very painful). However, the next day went much better and the concert was a huge success. There were about 15,000 people, we were told, sitting in the arena and all around on the lovely grassy hills which surround the Forum. I can't describe the thrill of taking that long walk around the orchestra to and from the piano with all those thousands standing and cheering.

Immediately backstage, Mr. Fiedler asked, 'The ending was all right, wasn't it?' I didn't have the heart to tell him that it was still too fast.

A wonderful thing happened — many people came backstage for autographs and Mr. Fiedler and I were seated at a table. He just signed his name (because, of course, he's signed so many thousands of autographs during his lifetime); but I'm still terribly flattered when someone wants my

*autograph so I usually ask the person's name and make it out personally,
"with Best Wishes" etc. At one point, Mr. Fiedler glanced over to see why it
was taking me so long to sign each autograph and to my amusement, I heard
him start to ask everyone his or her name!*

A nice little perk, off the regular path for Sheila, was being a regular
panelist on the CBC radio series, "Music and Opinion" — the panel comprised
moderator Don Newlands, music critic for the *Toronto Star*, William Littler,
Sheila, and a musical guest. It was a sort of quiz-cum-discussion-and-record
show, and there were 26 of them. Sheila was a witty woman and loved to talk;
she thoroughly enjoyed the work! Over the entire 26 shows, two guests stood
out in her mind: Aaron Copland and Jennie Tourel (who died of cancer about
two months after the show).

Everyone was quite jittery about meeting Mr. Copland, Sheila wrote
in her diary-cum-journal, *but I think he was more frightened than any of
us (although he tried hard not to show it). There is something about a
microphone that can tend to make one* freeze. *However, once relaxed he was a
charming guest with a dry wit. I remember "cutely" remarking that there
indeed were two sides to Aaron Copland (referring to his popular works and
his lesser-known 'serious' works), to which he replied, "Yes, a right side and a
left side".*

*Jennie Tourel died of cancer barely two months after she was on our
show. It was such a shock, no one knew she was ill, not even a Toronto pupil
who had studied with her for two years and came to hear the show. I was much
impressed with Miss Tourel's warmth and lack of pretense and her very real
love of music and great understanding of it. There was nothing of the prima
donna about her. I was very grateful for the opportunity of meeting her — a
great lady. I'm sorry this show is no longer on the air but perhaps it will be
revived some day in the future.* As an after-thought, Sheila added — *But, then,
who knows what the future will bring? This is what makes my life continually
exciting. The path of any artist is strewn with frustrations and disappointments
but they are more than outweighed by the rewards — not material, but
spiritual. I hope I have and will, in some small way, continue to enrich
people's lives with my music.*

This year had been a good one for Sheila, musically, but it also brought the
passing of her mother, finally, after 12 years of "vegetating" as a result of the
brain hemorrhage just before Sheila went to Geneva. Even though Sheila and
her father had been expecting her death at any time — and they couldn't
communicate at all with her during those years — they tended to put the
inevitable out of their minds. She had been, in a sense, still part of their lives.
Grief does strange things to us, Sheila wrote. *We cry openly for a while and
when we have no tears left, our hearts weep in silence.* Mr. Henig took his wife's

death very hard — perhaps a bit surprising under the circumstances — and Sheila felt her father's depression very keenly. *My poor father, he seems completely broken up. What can I do to help him at a time like this, when I myself so desperately need help.*

The year also brought the death of her beloved Lassie, the vow she had made so many years ago when her first puppy, Tiger, was killed, she never kept. She always had animals around her, and in maturity, she was able to accept with a certain peacefulness the fact that they would come and go out of her life.

My beautiful Lassie had a malignant tumor, and was put to sleep by the Humane Society. I now have a French poodle, his name is Peppe. He is very affectionate and cuddly, but not too bright, as compared to Lassie. Still, I love him. How can one not love an animal? When I'm practicing he makes himself comfortable on my piano bench beside me and falls asleep. Or he watches the children when he is awake. He is very playful and follows me wherever I go. If I don't take him, he sits down and cries like a baby. Last winter, on a very cold morning, I drove my children to school, and when I returned home, I found a small kitten curled up in a corner outside my kitchen door. I took it inside, fed it some warm milk, and realized that the kitten was sick. I drove down to a vet, and later nursed it until it got better. It was then that I was faced with a problem. I couldn't make up my mind what to do with it. I was in no position to adopt it since I already had three cats of my own, and wouldn't think of throwing it out of the house. I then decided to put an ad in a Toronto newspaper in which I said that I was looking for a good home for a cute and playful kitten. I was surprised by the response I received. The telephone hardly stopped ringing that day. I arranged to interview a couple who had one child, to make sure that they were nice people. After they came down to my house and had a cup of tea with me, I was convinced that the kitten was going to a good home.

To me, animals are very special and I don't wear anything trimmed with fur.

March, 1974, and a dream of Sheila's, oft times mentioned to anyone who would listen, came true. She staged a triumphant, if belated, homecoming to Winnipeg where she had been born and made headlines as "baby Sheila" but had never performed as a professional pianist. The homecoming consisted of a live solo recital at the University of Manitoba followed by a nationwide CBC broadcast with the CBC Winnipeg Orchestra the next day.

Winnipeg still enjoyed good times. The only part of town which had missed out on the good times was Sheila's birthplace, the north end, which had now become a shantytown inhabited by the native Indian population. It was a sad moment for Sheila, for she hated ghettoes, even the idea of them, and like many people of compassionate nature, felt deeply saddened by the inequality of the native people in comparison to the rest of Canadians, yet frustrated because the problems seem too enormous for them to do anything about it. It did not deter her enthusiasm for performing in her hometown, but, she said, "I don't like to think of these streets where I went back and forth from school, music lessons, dancing lessons — all that work and learning! —housing such a sad state of affairs."

On the Sunday afternoon, at the University of Manitoba, Sheila performed to a packed house Chopin's *B-Flat Minor Sonata*, the Prokofieff *Sonata* again, Schumann's *Pantheon,* and several intermezzi by Brahms. The next day, she went to the CBC studio to tape, under the direction of Arthur Polson, Cesar Franck's *Symphonic Variations*, a late nineteenth century work which Sheila felt, again, had been unnecessarily neglected, to be aired nationally. The press coverage of the recital was excellent — rave reviews again — and the Women's Musical Club invited her to return again, to perform with cellist Daniel Domb of the TSO. Sheila's friends, Harold and Ann Lugsdin, who had organized the concert at the University, also put the energy into promoting the Henig-Domb recital. However, it was not to happen for Daniel Domb's management would not release him from previous TSO commitments for the scheduled time. It was postponed.

The return home may have been anti-climactic for Sheila for although she was delighted to be in Winnipeg, particularly as a performing artist, much had changed there and much had changed in herself. But she could never go home again to stay; for better or worse, if she wished to stay in Canada, Toronto was Canada's cultural centre, it was her real home now, and Toronto was where she had to 'make it'.

Sheila was about to record what would become her most popular recording, certainly the most popular in terms of press coverage. The Canadian Talent Library organization, under the leadership of Lymon Potts, records Canadian performing artists of all persuasions, and the resulting albums are usually given airplay over at least the Standard Broadcast System, Canada's largest private radio network, with its flagship stations CFRB and CKFM in Toronto. Mal Thompson, former production chief of the Canadian Talent Library first approached Sheila in 1968 and asked her to do a record for them — CFRB had a two-hour light classical broadcast outlet. Mal had had extensive experience in Britain's broadcasting and recording industries and he recognized and promoted first-rate performers from jazz singer Salome Bey to big-band trombonist Teddy Rodderman to Sheila Henig. The album was recorded, sold to the London label and featured what trade magazine critic Bernard Thorne described as "one of the finest recordings of Debussy's *Claire de Lune* I have heard". The album also contained Brahm's *Intermezzo in C Major* (which Thorne praised for its "gay, spirited rendering"), *Four Preludes* by Srul Glick, Rachmaninoff's *Prelude in G Major* and two *Etudes* by Chopin as well as his *Waltz in A Flat*. Except for an occasional airplay over Starlight Serenade and a few of its equivalents, few people even knew of the record's existence, and the

Toronto press had taken no note of it at all. It was not a very encouraging event in Sheila's life.

Two years later, the Canadian Radio and Television Commission (CRTC) headed by Pierre Juneau, passed a key ruling that a certain percentage of all programming on all radio stations had to be Canadian in origin, whether it be written, performed or, in some cases, the majority of technical crew and backup band/orchestra. While folk singers and rock bands reaped the greatest benefit from the ruling, and there were strong objections from a few major pop stations, there were those perceptive enough, and genuinely interested enough in promoting good Canadian talent, that they utilized the new ruling which meant a certain amount of guaranteed airplay, and tried to create a thriving local scene involving all types of performers, all kinds of music.

The CRTC rulings gave Sheila, and many others, a brand new opportunity. As Sheila herself explained in an interview after the record, *Piano Portraits*, was released, "I hadn't done anything for Canadian Talent Library for six and a half years, and was tired of hearing the same old record, so I dropped a note to Mal Thompson and suggested making a new one. To my pleasant surprise, he said, 'Sure', and we set up a date for April 1975. You never know, though, whether a commercial label will pick up one of these records, so I got a brain wave."

Sheila had a friend, Toller Cranston, world champion figure skater, winner of the 1972 Winter Olympics, the world's free-skating champion of 1974 and '75, and so many championships that they are literally too numerous to count. His dramatic ice-choreography and startling performing style brought him raves from all over the world as the most original and exciting skater ever: "Nureyev on ice", he was called. He is also an accomplished painter and has had exhibitions of his work in Montreal, Toronto, Dusseldorf, Munich and throughout Australia.

"I had shown an exhibition of paintings by Toller Cranston at my house while doing a preview for the Toronto Symphony Women's Committee," Sheila explained in an interview, "and called him to ask if he wouldn't mind my using one of them for an album jacket. I took the print to Mal and suggested he go to Attic Records, a small but active record company, with the whole thing as a package. They bought it. And now, London is distributing it." Sheila was learning that the way to success is always easier if paved with a good promotional idea.

The painting by Cranston was a portrait of a debonair, flamboyant Mediterranean lady crowned with an elaborate magenta-blue floral fedora, holding up a black rococo tiara. Her long full dress is white with elegant red embroidery around the waist, partially covered in soft magenta pansies which almost seem to flutter. The initial impression is a very sensual portrait of an intriguing woman, but under close inspection, the detail is executed with almost clinical precision, and the expression on the lady's thin, tight lips is totally frozen. This painting, plus the music, comprised the title of the album, *Piano Portraits.*

It was recorded under the best studio conditions in downtown Toronto's Manta Sound Studio with Sheila using Anton Kuerti's piano. At the same time, Canadian Talent Library was recording two other albums, of totally diverse music styles, in the same studio: Jackie Mittoo, a Jamaican reggae singer was working on his album, and middle-of-the-road pop pianist Hagood Hardy was recording *Homecoming* which would, six months later, become a million-seller across the continent.

Mal Thompson couldn't praise Sheila enough — she worked very hard on the album, was extremely cooperative, and when it was completed, did everything possible to promote it, even to writing the program notes on the jacket, which are reproduced here in their entirety.

1. The Brahms *Ballade in G Minor* is the third of six short pieces comprising Opus 118. It combines the best features of Brahms — opening and closing sections have great strength and energy while the middle section is flowing and lyrical. The final bars (based on the theme from the middle section) are plaintive and questioning.

2. The *Impromptu in G Flat* is so typically Schubertian that I think one could guess the composer after only a few bars. It is one of his best-known piano works but, as in so many of his lyrical works, it could easily be sung with piano accompaniment. It is, indeed, a "song without words" — dream-like and tender, disturbed occasionally by a passionate outburst of emotion.

3. The *Andante and Rondo Capriccioso* is Mendelssohn at his best. The short opening is a gorgeous song, followed by a delicious Scherzo-like movement. There was no composer who could write a Scherzo as could Felix Mendelssohn. (Think of his famous Scherzo from his Octet.) This work is a joy to performer and audience alike.

4. The *Nocturne in C Minor* is totally unlike any of the other Chopin nocturnes. It has never achieved the popularity of some of the other nocturnes because it lacks, perhaps, the easily accessible sentimentality of the others. It is, indeed, tragic and noble — the opening section is like a Pavane with its steady and continuous bass accompaniment underlying a hauntingly poignant melody. This leads to a somewhat slower, chorale-like section which, becoming more impassioned, leads into the final "Doppio Movimento" section (which is the opening melody accompanied by agitated triplets). The last few bars return to the mood of the opening — the final chords, almost resigned but not quite (questioning perhaps). A magnificient miniature music drama; unduly neglected, I feel.

5. The *C Minor Etude* is the final one of Opus 25, and a fitting finale it is, too. It is short but physically demanding for the performer as there is no let-up in the constant flow of grandiose arpeggios. It ends in C major with a glorious pealing of bells in the left hand. The work is rugged and tumultuous — "Chopin the conqueror!"

6. The *Sonatine* by Ravel shows the composer's love for the old masters. (Note also his "Tombeau de Couperin"). It is literally a small sonata

and is in the classical three-movement form. The first movement is marked "doux et expressif" and, although not quite in Ravel's normally impressionistic style, is full of his delicious harmonies. The second movement is an exquisite Minuet which slows down gradually into a very broad ending. The last movement is a brilliant tour-de-force for the pianist — almost like a toccata except for the two brief lyrical sections and it ends in a blaze of fireworks. The entire work is a miniature gem.

7. Poulenc's *Pastourelle* is a delightful work — charming and unsentimental, with a saucy tongue-in-cheek ending that typifies so much of this composer's writing. This work is part of a ballet suite, "L'Evantail de Jeanne" (Joan's Fan) which was made up of a number of French composers' works (including Darius Milhaud and Maurice Ravel).

8. *Serenade* by Richard Strauss is one of the most beautiful of all German Lieder. Originally for voice and piano, this arrangement for piano solo by the late Walter Gieseking captures the ecstatic vocal line with it's constantly rippling accompaniment. The opening words of the song — "Awake, arise, but softly, my love!" sets the mood of rapturous expectancy which leads to a glorious sunburst at the climax — "And the roses, awakened by morning's delight, shall glow with the wondrous bliss of the night."

9. The *Etude in E Major* is the fifth in Scriabin's early Opus 8 set of Piano Etudes. It is interesting to note that there are 12 Etudes; the same number as both Opus 10 and Opus 25 of Chopin. Scriabin was, in fact, much influenced by Chopin at this stage of development. (He lived, in his prime, about fifty years after Chopin.) There is nothing in this piece that even suggests the dark, brooding mysticism of his later works. It is marked "brioso" and is very buoyant and gracious with a declamatory middle-section.

10. The *Idyll* and *Scherzo-Valse* are from Chabrier's "Pieces Pittoresques" for piano. The composer instructs the pianist to play the Idyll with freshness and simplicity while the Scherzo-Valse is a very brilliant and rhythmically exciting work. All of Chabrier's music seems full of sunshine, yet, towards the end of his life, he became the victim of acute melancholia bordering on insanity.

To many of her colleagues, *Piano Portraits* seemed to sum up the essence of Sheila: polished, jewel-like piano works, technically intricate yet sublimely romantic — unusually luminescent, graciously civilized beauty *par excellence*.

For once, at last, Sheila's efforts received good coverage from the *Toronto Star* and the *Toronto Sun,* as well as a warmly intelligent review from the Vancouver "underground" weekly, *Georgia Straight.*

... SHEILA PERFORMS MASTERFULLY IN ATTIC
Vancouver, October 2, 1975
Georgia Straight

Mal Thompson, who produced Sheila's best known album, *Piano Portraits*.

SHEILA HENIG: PIANO PORTRAITS: Works by Brahms, Schubert, Chopin, Ravel, Poulenc, Richard Strauss, Scriabin, Chabrier, Sheila Henig/piano, Attic LAT1002.

Sometimes it pays not to read your mail.

When this record arrived, it came with a letter and the usual volume of liner notes on the back of a jacket.

Instead of reading, I simply put the disc on the stereo and went back to fiddling around with the typewriter. Then I stopped, turned around, leaned back and let the music occupy me completely.

What I heard was a well thought out and nicely balanced series of short piano masterpieces, beginning with the Ballade in G Minor, Opus 118 No. 3, by Brahms, followed by Schubert's Impromptu in G-flat Major, opus 90 No. 3, then the Andante and Rondo Capriccioso by Mendelssohn, Chopin's Nocturne in C minor, opus 48 No. 1, and his C minor Etude, opus 25, No. 12, and so forth.

More than that, I heard a pianist with the unusual gift to bring out the poetic beauty of the music and yet be assertive and powerful. The tone was not familiar, but it was obviously that of an understanding artist with great technical mastery and the musical maturity and insight to go beyond mere technique to find the personality of the music and shape it within the acceptable bounds to the personality of the performer.

Aside from all the factors of piano playing that can be defined and analyzed, however, the performance had that elusive quality which you can't put your finger on precisely but which is very important in making a record, one to be savored and played again and again: It felt good, was comfortable to live with.

When I finally read the letter and liner-notes, I discovered that the artist is a Canadian woman and the label — Attic — a Canadian company. Sheila Henig graduated as an Eaton award winner at the University of Toronto Faculty of Music, was named a Laureate at the Geneva International Competitions and has toured Europe and the U.S. to great acclaim.

It's always nice to be accidently unbiased.

William Littler of the *Toronto Star* used the advent of the album to offer cryptic comments on the state of classical recordings in general, but also threw Sheila some backhanded compliments for determination. He was perhaps one of the few music critics to recognize and publicize precisely the kind of toughness needed to survive in the classical music business.

PIANIST'S ART ADDS TO DISC TREASUREHOUSE

Sheila Henig happens to be the lucky exception among Canadian artists; she has just had not one but two long playing records released and the lady is understandably pleased.

Pleased but realistic. These aren't her first albums — they are her third and fourth — and she still remembers the 75-cent royalty cheque the earlier ones earned her. She refers to that album as the best kept secret of 1968. . . .

Miss Henig has learned the hard way that the road to riches is not paved in vinyl. The classical record market produces few million sellers, and if it weren't for those twin fairy god-mothers, the Canadian Broadcasting Corporation and the Canadian Radio-Television Commission, she and many of her colleagues might never be invited into a studio.

LADIES BOUNTIFUL

In fact, she can thank those ladies bountiful for the chance to make both of her new discs. Attic's Sheila Henig Piano Portraits (LAT 1002) originated as a Canadian Talent Library album for use by radio stations anxious to fill their Canadian content quotas. The CBC Vancouver Chamber Orchestra with Sheila Henig (SM205) is one of 56 new releases in the CBC's Canadian collection.

In a truer sense, though, the Toronto pianist can thank herself for the existence of these recordings. Unlike some of her less determined fellow ivoryhunters, she has realized that a career must be worked for.

Married to a pharmacist and the mother of two children she could fill her days with things other than six or seven hours of practicing. Not sure why she lets herself get tied up in knots at the prospect of performing, she even went through analysis for a while. The only answer she has come up with is that the love of performing is in her blood.

Whatever put it there, it has made Sheila Henig not only a Geneva International Competition prize winner, but the kind of artist who will go after an engagement or a recording without waiting around to be asked.

Littler then quoted Sheila on how she went about getting the recording made in the first place, approaching Mal Thompson and getting the Cranston painting.

The gestation of the CBC record took longer. As Miss Henig tells it, "I had been trying to interest people in recording the Healey Willan Concerto ever since I first learned it in 1965. It's a gorgeous work.

"But the recording seems almost to have been jinxed. When I was asked to go out to Vancouver to record it with John Avison and the CBC Chamber Orchestra, I wound up in a car accident.

"Then, when we did the recording, the engineers didn't like the sound and I had to go back and re-tape it. When I listened to both tapes the first was actually better than the second, so I said: 'It has to be the first one!' "

Needless to say, the version on SM205 turned out to be the one Miss Henig liked. And an important addition to the recorded library of Canadian music it is, too.

And speaking of this library, the CBC's Canadian Collection, of which it is a part, constitutes a veritable treasurehouse of Canadian music and musicians. It's a pity the discs are available only by mail (at $5 each plus postage from CBC Publications, Box 500, Station A, Toronto M5W 1E6, from whom a free catalogue can be obtained).

A pity indeed! And one begins to understand why Canadian musicians have such a tough time getting their work before the public when their "treasurehouses" are not available to the public in the public marketplace but must be written for, money paid in advance before receipt of the record, and no one even knows about it unless they listen to the CBC or a Bill Littler comes along and tells them about it and how to go about getting it. How could one hope to make the Canadian public aware of their own artists if their work is sequestered for an elite minority. For sure the CBC has somewhere, in the small print of their mandate, a reason why these recordings are unavailable to the public in the normal retail fashion, but does it make any sense? Sheila herself would bitterly remark about this kind of frustration. "You lose your positive, aggressive way of thinking. Eventually your confidence begins to dwindle and you are terrified you'll give up in disgust and fall by the wayside."

It wasn't until December, 1975 that Wilder Penfield III of the *Toronto Sun* got around to mentioning both of Sheila's records, but he used it to alert Toronto that Sheila was off on another European tour (a small one this time).

> On the basis of these credits [the records], Sheila Henig has to be the most successful female classical pianist in Canada.
> But it would not allow her to survive for a month without subsidies from the CBC, the CTL and her pharmacist husband.

Sheila talked to Penfield about her "first love", singing. "To me the human voice is the most beautiful of instruments. Nothing can move me to tears like vocal recital by a great artist — it's a much more direct means of communication than the piano."

'But she still has a dream,' Penfield wrote. '— one day she would like to accompany her own lieder recital. (So far, the closest she has come was singing "You'll Never Walk Alone" on CBC radio while backing herself on the piano.)

'In the meantime, the challenges she faces on the piano alone are more than enough to sustain her interest.'

Sheila talked to Penfield of these challenges, one of them being, according to Sheila, her own fear. Acclaim from abroad did nothing to lessen the tension. "I used to think my nervousness would decrease when I got more experience. It doesn't, it gets worse as your reputation gets better, maybe because you have farther to fall."

She told Penfield that, at the moment, she was feeling lucky. "I have a psychic friend who told me my picture was going to be on the cover of Time magazine in 1978. An astrologer has told me the next few years will be incredibly good."

'Furthermore,' Penfield wrote, 'her chart has told her tomorrow is going to be a good day and that February will be an exceptionally good month. . . .'

> Sure, these may be psychological crutches. Behind the charm and cheer of her optimism is a bundle of nervous energy. But it doesn't take a sixth sense to let you know that the woman of Piano Portraits and the Willan Concerto is an exceptional musician.
> Listening is believing.

Public appreciation of classical music does exist, of course. It does not necessarily have to rely upon government agencies such as the CBC and CRTC. In Minneapolis-St. Paul, where such agencies don't exist, Larry Roberts of WAYL-radio wrote to Mal Thompson: "If your albums (in the future) are as good as the ones you last sent [referring to Piano Portraits] we may have to annex the Twin Cities to Canada!"

The initial excitement over the release of Piano Portraits inspired Sheila and Toller Cranston to work together on a TV project which would have featured both their talents in a most exciting concept. Titled "Music on Ice" Toller would choreograph ice ballets to Sheila's performances of piano works. Sheila jumped into this project with all her heart — she had always been a great admirer of Cranston. "To watch Toller performing is like listening to angels singing, or trying to touch the wind. His interpretation, emotional, so dramatic, always brings tears to my eyes. He seems to be reaching out to infinity, and he succeeds."

Sheila presented the proposal to CBC producer Mario Prizek, and added, besides herself and Toller Cranston, that perhaps the Toronto Symphony could be involved too, making the entire concept a super-special. Prizek was, initially, enthusiastic. But the CBC hemmed and hawed, ultimately cancelling the proposal. Mario Prizek, when interviewed, stated the program was turned down for budgetary reasons: it would involve two departments, the serious music department and the variety department, and the two of them couldn't get a cross-pollination happening so that the budget of one (variety) would help feed the limited budget of the other (serious music). Sometime later, Cranston did a special on the CBC without Sheila and in a much more pop-oriented format. This proposal was successful because it was presented to the variety department by a private sponsor, rather than the serious music department, for which Prizek works.

Prizek felt badly about the loss of the proposed show: "In any single season we have the funds for only a very few new 'spectaculars' — e.g. ballets, operas, symphony concerts, musical documentaries, etc. The remainder of the season has to be made up of 'repeats' from previous seasons. In the year in which I presented the suggestion which Toller, Sheila and I had formulated, John Barnes (the head of the music department) had almost completely committed those limited resources to other projects. He saw the merit in our ideas, but his hands were tied (at least for the whole of the following production year)."

"I have no accurate information," he continued in his written account to a query, "as to how the Variety Department came to do Toller's show; I can only speculate that the show, in its changed format, was presented to the CBC by the agency which was handling the sponsor's accounts, in which case its format would be determined largely by the wishes of that sponsor and the audience they wished to reach."

Sheila was to be deeply hurt by what seemed a betrayal — by whom and under what circumstances she would never know. It just seemed that all the energy and the creative plotting that she had gone through to realize the project had been taken from her and used for other people's benefit. Not a bitter woman by nature, she would allude to this episode in bitterness.

In the meantime, *Piano Portraits* — and the upcoming European tour — seemed to sustain her. She suggested to interviewer Linda West (in the Oscapella Concerts blurb, her management agency) that the album had saved her from a nervous breakdown — "I was as close to a nervous breakdown as I ever want to come," she stated. "I really feel the album has been my baby from start to finish. That's why I'm so excited about it." Linda West continued:

> But a career as a concert pianist isn't easy and being a woman doesn't make it any easier. There are the long hours of practice which must be worked around the responsibilities of being a wife and mother. And of course there are the inevitable "catastrophies" that happen right before a concert — a housekeeper leaves or one of the children comes down with chicken pox. Long tours are out of the question too, because Henig doesn't like to take that much time away from her family.
>
> "It's almost impossible to make a living in this business unless you are prepared to spend weeks on the road touring," she said.
>
> One way of making money is through teaching. Henig has given private lessons from time to time and she expects that her retirement from the concert stage will lead her to some form of university post. That's still far in the distant future. Now, with a revived spirit and a career that is moving ahead, Henig is too excited about the present to worry about the future.

A longer article in Audio Scene Canada, (February 1976, Patricia O'Leary) allowed Sheila to elaborate on the personal problems of being an artist, a professional woman, and a mother. She was asked, "With so many talented pianists around, what makes one person able and willing to become a concert soloist?"

"Absolute determination," said Sheila. "I think that counts almost more than talent. And luck, and timing are important too." Sheila mentioned that artists have bad periods, too, and it is at those times when you either hang in or give up. She herself was considering quitting a couple of years ago.

"There were very few concerts, no recordings, just the odd broadcast, and I had to have a long talk with myself to see if it was really worth all the hard work." Whether there was something to work towards or not, she still had to put in six hours a day practicing, she told Ms. O'Leary.

"I even went into therapy for a while, to see why I was going through all this. I've come to the conclusion that too much self-analysis isn't a good thing anyway, but I decided that I must love performing enough to go on. And strangely enough, right after that low time everything seemed to break. I became so busy for the next six months that I couldn't even take a day off."

Sheila Henig is not one to sit back and let the work come to her.

"I hate to say it, but you do have to be pushy. There are only so many jobs available, and while as a woman it goes against the grain sometimes, in this business you do have to be aggressive."

Talking about the *Piano Portraits* album, Sheila said, "I've been promoting that record myself, and in one commercial I said, 'If you don't like the music you can always frame the jacket,' which was meant to be entirely tongue-in-cheek. Some people asked what I was doing knocking my own playing! But it wasn't meant to be that way at all."

Patricia O'Leary noted that Sheila was physically a small woman but was known for the strong clear sound she produced on the piano. "People have asked me, especially in Europe when I've played there, how a small person like me gets so much sound. But it's not how big you are that counts, it's how you produce your tone." Consistency of practising was important to build up stamina, she felt. Sheila, herself, didn't do any special physical exercises to keep fit, only some relaxation ones to ease the tension in her neck.

Sheila told the interviewer that she didn't have any particular philosophy and that she didn't, consciously anyway, try to impose her personality on the music.

"I try to decide what the composer is saying, and I attempt to play it as clearly and directly as possible. Usually, as I work on a piece, it somehow clarifies itself. And a piece grows. For instance, I played the Liszt B Minor Sonata several years ago and put it away for four years. Then I recently revived it for a concert; and when I realized how I used to play certain passages, I thought 'Did I play it like that? Well, I don't like it that way now'. And you can hear differences with pieces by people like Horowitz or Rubenstein that they recorded 30 years ago and then did again more recently."

February, 1976, and Sheila was back in Europe — very briefly this time. The tour went from Brussels to Rotterdam, then to Vienna and Saltzburg. It proved one indisputable fact, Sheila was no one-shot morning glory, for this time she got unequivocal raves. She played the *Scherzo* again (Morawetz) plus works by Chopin, Schumann and Liszt. The Saltzburger *Volksblatt* (for her performance at the Viennese Hall of the Mozarteum) said of her performance of the *Scherzo* — "Here . . . she was able to make full use of her remarkable skills. Her playing had a pearly, flowing effect. The musical piece was interpreted lively and unimpaired — with genuine joy. This contribution can clearly be called the climax of the concert."

The *Berchtesgadener Anzeiger* agreed (Feb. 25, 1967) and called the *Scherzo* "a musically exquisite item". The reviewer picked out Chopin's *Sonata in B-flat Minor* (opus 35) and the Liszt *Sonata in B-Minor* for special attention. "After she had given evidence already of a musicality that is proficient in style when playing the Schumann cycle, she added a virtuoso element when playing the famous Chopin sonata. Her technical skills permitted her to interpret the basic movements and the scherzo with a genuinely romantic bravura. . . .

> By mistake the last piece on the program shown on the posters was a Sonata in B-flat minor by Liszt; actually it was the Sonata in B-Minor; one could not get over one's amazement at the bravura with which this piano work was performed, a work which is important to every pianist of rank. Here again, Sheila Henig did not compromise with the tempi where prestissimo octaves require the highest virtuosity toward the end of the piece. This piano night was poorly attended. This was unfortunate because one could listen to two of the most significant piano works in concert literature through an uncompromising performance by an outstanding pianist.

Returning home, the Toronto press published nothing about the tour, although she was interviewed. One year later, Sid Adelman in his "Eye on Entertainment" column (*Toronto Star*) gave her this mention:

PLUCKY PIANIST PULLS THROUGH
Picture this scene. Toronto classical pianist Sheila Henig is giving a major recital in Rotterdam while on a European tour. During the final moments of a Liszt sonata, she gets a tickle in her throat and starts coughing uncontrollably. She manages to stifle the cough, but tears come to her eyes. The piece finishes and she rushes backstage into a coughing fit. An appreciative audience jumps to its feet and shouts for more. She comes back for three encores; the coughing subsided. "It was just unreal," she says back in Toronto. "Ironically, it was the best performance of the tour, and I got the best reviews there. I can laugh about it now." That concert was tinged with danger from the start. Playing a Chopin piece, Henig was interrupted by a loudspeaker inadvertently left on, and blaring out mutterings from backstage.

More and more Sheila wondered, what do I have to do to get proper recognition at home? She clipped Adelman's notice and sent it to a friend, along with this remark in bold, angry hand-writing. "The reason I'm drawing your attention to the article is the timing. It took him all that time to get around to writing it. This only proves how people in the music world think. They are forever living in the woodwork when something good happens to an artist."

Perhaps the only thing that saved Sheila from total defeat in the wake of a highly successful trip to Europe which went unnoticed was that she surrounded herself with people who kept trying to make things happen.

The year 1977 was not a vintage year for anybody, anywhere, except for perhaps the notoriety of world problems, but Sheila kept trying. Among those kindred souls she kept reaching out to was Michel l'Esperance, a young Quebec composer whose very name means "hope". He himself wrote of their communications and single meeting, an understated, almost frighteningly moving account of the awful frustration in the struggle to get exciting creative ideas into the world of reality.

"In 1975, my music studies had been over for more than a year; and as a composer I was deeply involved in writing musicals. My creative energies ran from classics to jazz. I was faced with the problem of definition.

"At that time, in hopes of acquiring funding for production of a (stage) musical, I approached Polygram Records. It was a bit confusing. I got interest from two different departments. First, the classical artists-and-repertory man was trying to convince me of pursuing my classical writing (Vas Polakis). Secondly, Michael Hoppee of the middle-of-the-road department felt that I should reach for that market. On the basis of one of my songs, which I played for him, he felt there was substantial potential.

"By late 1976 I was working hard at both fields. I was feeling much anxiety and confusion. During a conversation with Joanne Ruderfer (co-producer of the stage musical, "Keeping Company") she suggested that I get in touch with Sheila.

"I phoned Sheila from Montreal and that evening we discussed at length the performances of new Canadian works. She was most interested and receptive. I found her to be not only sympathetic to that idea, but also frustrated herself at the lack of opportunity for "classical" performers. We agreed that I would send her my latest work.

"It is called *The Rich*, and is a short piece for piano and orchestra. It was written as a comment on the pains and "blues" that surely must be part of the wealthy. I discussed the emotional intent and my attitude behind the piece. She was enthusiastic and so I sent it to her.

"A week later, she called and was concerned with one of the passages. I explained it to her and then talked more about the whole piece.

"Sheila wanted us to meet, and she would then play it for me. In February 1977 I took a train to Toronto and she met me at the station. I remember her being nervous, strange. I was feeling the same thing. It was the first time we met, but it seemed like we had known each other well by the end of the day. When we got in the car she talked and talked about everything. It was a beautiful sunny day, but cold as hell.

"We went to the Royal Conservatory on Bloor Street. She had arranged for us to be in a hall by ourselves. I don't wish to get melodramatic, but it was like a scene from a movie. The sun was shining through the windows at an angle that shone just behind Sheila as she sat at the piano. She told me that she enjoyed the music and hoped her performance would be good. Well, she played with a sensitivity and sureness that almost had me in tears. I mean, she just played in a way that I could not have asked for more. As a writer and musician, I find that technique is fairly available from most accomplished musicians, but that expression is often at a loss. Sheila simply had both.

"When she finished, she asked if this was all right. I had to cut her off and say that it was wonderful.

"I was happy and so was she. We went to a nearby restaurant for lunch. As we walked, our conversation was about the possibilities of somehow performing my work. That kind of talk, I find, always gets depressing when you get to the nitty-gritty of getting something like that done. It did.

"Sheila was hoping for an upcoming concert with the Toronto Symphony. It was not yet confirmed, and she said she was getting fed up with the constant "run-a-round" she was getting.

"Another possibility was doing an album with Attic Records. She had already done one and praised the people of that organization. She made a point that Toller Cranston had done the painting for her record jacket. She was very proud. Over lunch, Sheila gave me a copy and I asked her to autograph it.

"We discussed another possibility for doing a joint project, me writing and her playing. We thought that maybe the Canada Council could help with the funding. But we eventually agreed that the idea was too "logical" and made too much sense for the Canada Council to get involved. We share in that cynical approach.

"Sheila impressed me in that she had many frustrations and yet appeared persistant. During lunch, she told me of her prouder moments: concerts that kept her feeling strong and helped her continue. At one point, she made comparison of herself with an old woman concert pianist. I wish I could be more specific, but I can't remember her name. Anyway, Sheila was speaking about the difficulties of women competing with men. She felt that she was as capable as any man in performing with expression and "power". She agreed when I suggested that maybe certain pieces requiring excessive handspread might be physically impossible for women because of their smaller hands.

"On this point of competition, Sheila was not optimistic about herself against seemingly impossible odds. At this point of our conversation, I tried pointing out that to be an artist was often lonely and frustrating and to be a part of the music world as she had been, to date, was already more than most can hope for.

"Our lunch had to end as I had a train to catch. Sheila drove me back to Union Station and as we went, she said she would try with Attic Records and the Toronto Symphony.

"Our luncheon had been informative, intimate and certainly was inspiring. On my way back to Montreal, I found myself even more confused about my own writing, since Sheila had made me feel so good.

"As the weeks passed, we phoned each other a few times and briefly went over the lack of progress on both of our parts.

"As time went on, Sheila and I lost track of each other. She sent me a letter a few months later, but that was it.

(November 1979)
"I am now completely involved in contemporary music: middle-of-the-

road and rock n' roll. For the time being, I found myself musically. I would hope to one day return to the music Sheila so warmly played. However, I cannot live that way at present."[1]

Sheila's involvement with Temple Emanu-El was the only consistant musical support she had during the '70s. Amy Gilbert, director of the Temple choir and Daniel Domb's wife, was also one of Sheila's close friends. "She was wonderfully generous," Amy recounts, "she was genuinely concerned with me," referring to the help Sheila gave her when Amy's babies were born. Her involvement was musical and social, for Rabbi Arthur Bielfeld remembers her "born desire to teach". She had an easy relationship with her fellow choir members and seemed unconcerned that they were not professionals. In fact, the Rabbi recalls, she was very careful not to impress them with her expertise for she was very conscious of the hurt that could be done to these dedicated people if she tried in any way to push her professional weight around. For the most part, she simply enjoyed the camaraderie and the mutual involvement in the music.

Temple Emanu-El was a reform synagogue but continued traditional observances, to a degree, and definitely encouraged the creation and preservation of the Jewish musical culture, adapting serious classical and contemporary music from the surrounding secular society to utilize them as vehicles for new innovative forms of authentic Jewish musical prayer expression. Amy was a great aid here for her experience was by no means confined to Jewish music; she had worked with such notable choirmasters as Robert Shaw and Julius Rudel and had even conducted Penderecki's *St. Luke's Passion* under the auspices of Shaw. When Amy was occupied with giving birth to her children, Sheila doubled as conductor.

Here, at the Temple, regardless of the ups and downs she experienced in the professional world of music, she felt, musically, most at home, most eager to give of herself freely and able to experiment and further develop her skills. She worked with Amy on the repertoire which included not only works by Ernest Bloch, but also modern Jewish religious compositions by avant garde American composers such as Charles Davidson and Max Janowsky, as well as Toronto contemporaries Ben Steinberg, Srul Glick and Milton Barnes. Sheila's involvement made use of all her musical capacities — choirmember, soloist and piano accompaniment.

Sheila herself was never very vocal about her religious feelings and beliefs, but her father felt that the Temple gave her great sustenance and a sense of belonging — not just musically — to a group with which she identified. The feeling amongst Jews the world over was one of unease in the mid-70s as the increasing Arab oil-based economic muscle was flexing itself at the energy-hungry world. It also gave her a chance to sing in an essentially non-professional environment, out of the eye of the media. She did choose, however,

[1] We wish to extend our personal thanks to Toronto theatrical producer Joanne Ruderfer for linking us up directly to Michel l'Esperance who supplied us with these notes of personal recollection of Sheila.

116

once, to bring her sensibilities as a Jew out into the open, professionally. The International Women's Year (1975) celebration of Festival of Women and the Arts, organized by Toronto publicist and theatrical entrepreneur Vivienne Muhling, took place at the St. Lawrence Centre for the Arts, and Sheila was among the many women invited to take part. It was particularly fitting in this case for other professional women were doing likewise — jazz singer, Salome Bey proudly proclaimed her Black heritage while Selyani did much the same with her Macedonian background. The show comprised a host of 'known' female stars including folk singer Sylvia Tyson, actresses Kate Reid and Jane Mallett, revue artist Dinah Christie and the comedy team of Sandra O'Neill and Barbara Hamilton of "Sweet Reason". Sheila chose Annie Rutzky's *Scherzo for Piano* composed in 1942, one year before her death in Auschwitz. It was important for Sheila because of the situation and despair out of which the woman wrote the piece and she gave it a very moving performance, as Vivienne Muhling later remarked. Ms. Muhling was also pleasantly surprised by Sheila's cooperativeness and unpretentiousness, in contrast to the prima donna acts some of the other stars pulled. No special note was made of the piece or of Sheila's presence; the Globe sent its drama critic who took notice only of the actresses and revue artists and confessed that from his own selfish viewpoint, that's all he would like to have seen. But that was the first, and last, time that Sheila stepped out of her usual professional role as a musician for the general public. All of her concerts, broadcasts and recordings were based on the classical repertoire which she felt suited her particular talents.

Sheila's close friendship with Amy spilled over into a professional one with Amy's husband, Daniel Domb. The two of them gave a superb recital at the Edward Johnson Building (Walter Hall) in August of 1977. The concert was part of the CBC Summer Soiree series featuring the music of Edward Grieg, a key link between the strongly melodic late romanticism of Brahms and the impressionism of Debussy. Grieg is most popularly known for his *Peer Gynt Suite* and the *Piano Concerto in A Minor*. Sheila and Domb performed his *Sonata in A Minor for Cello and Piano*, while each took solo performances in other works. They later recorded the Grieg Sonata for the CBC Talent Library, but due to a union dispute, it was not released until December, 1980.

Sheila was in an innovative mood for her Carnegie Recital Hall debut in March, 1978. "I sought to do my recital differently. After all, the time of a straight solo recital is on the wane. People are looking for more variety. And I want to extend myself."

Extend herself she did. She transformed it into, to quote her directly "An Evening of Music" (the title she used for the recital). First, she performed in the dual role of singer and pianist, and she included in the program Russian-born virtuoso oboist, Senia Trubashnik, whom she had met in Toronto.

Trubashnik made his concert debut at 15, and was appointed a year later as oboe soloist with the Moscow Philharmonic. Unable to endure the anti-

Semitism and general cultural atmosphere within the Soviet Union, he emigrated to Toronto in 1976 and since then has appeared with some of the greatest conductors and performers in the world. He lived in Toronto during 1976 and 1977.

For months before the concert Sheila concentrated on her voice. She studied with Toronto vocal coach Elizabeth Benson-Guy at the Royal Conservatory; she sang for director of the music program at the St. Lawrence Centre, Franz Kramer, who saw possibilities in her voice but advised her that she could not do an entire vocal recital but rather one major group of songs as part of a piano recital. And finally, she worked with old friend Stuart Hamilton, seeking his advice on her choice of material and her interpretation and colouring of the piano accompaniment (she would accompany herself). Sheila, knowing her voice was not suitable for opera, chose works from the Lieder and renaissance repertoire and asked for Hamilton's opinion. They agreed upon a selection by Henry Purcell and the complete group of the Dvorak love songs, six in total. She used the original accompaniment score by Dvorak, and then she and Hamilton conferred again on her interpretation.

Her enthusiasm for the innovative and adventurous was put to the test in preparation for the concert. She herself couldn't recall working harder, or with more nervous energy, for any previous musical event in her life. "I've played in concert halls all over the world, but Carnegie gives me butterflies."

In early March, 1978, New York was still digging itself out of a heavy snowfall; it has a particular magic at these moments, it's unrelenting hum of traffic noise obliterated. The great city seems to be muffled in a soft blanket and it's ability to intimidate non-New Yorkers disappears.

The innovation, and the tremendous effort which went into making it a success, paid off. The New York *Times*, which she hoped and prayed would send a critic to the recital, sent their regular music critic, Joseph Horowitz, and he gave both Sheila and Senia Trubashnik a rave review.

Sheila Henig as Pianist
Singer, Chamber Artist
For her New York recital debut Thursday night at Carnegie Recital Hall, Sheila Henig performed as a solo pianist, a chamber musician and a singer. It was no stunt — Miss Henig, who graduated from the University of Toronto with degrees in piano and voice, left no doubt that she was a richly satisfying artist in all three capacities.

Miss Henig showed more than a little self-confidence by choosing the oboist Senia Trubashnik as her chamber-music partner in works by Poulenc, Schumann, Purcell and Oskar Morawetz. Mr. Trubashnik, who was principal oboist of the Moscow Chamber Orchestra before emigrating in 1976, would have thoroughly overshadowed a lesser pianist. He is a magnificient player, with a more colorfully pungent tone than is usually heard in the West, and an extraordinary ability to mold and inflect the line.

The high point of the evening was a strikingly romantic interpretation of the Poulenc Sonata for Oboe and Piano. Mr. Trubashnik's poignant songful approach employed rhythmic liberties not normally associated with such music, and Miss Henig furnished compelling support every step of the way. One was strongly reminded that Poulenc dedicated this splendid 1962 score to a Russian composer — Prokofieff.

As a solo pianist, Miss Henig was especially impressive in a boldly conceived, deliberately paced account of Liszt's "Funerailles." Her lightly pedalled performance of Schumann's "Papillons" was distinguished by unusually lucid textures, as well as the necessary impetuosity and wit. A couple of Chopin selections were surprisingly earthbound, however.

Finally, Miss Henig sang Dvorak's "Liebeslieder" (Op. 83). The sweet, quivery timbre of her soprano proved most appealing, and she accompanied herself with unfailing sensitivity. Even so, one could not help feeling that the singing would have been more communicative had Miss Henig been able to stand and face the audience.

After the recital, Trubashnik was on his way; he had left Toronto as a permanent residence the year before due to lack of suitable work opportunities.

When Sheila returned triumphantly from New York, the entire Canadian musical scene should have been her oyster.

It wasn't. In fact, even doors which had been opened to her before were now closing. She wrote her friends Ann and Harold Lugsdin in Winnipeg, mailing them some biographical information and reviews for a concert there (with Daniel Domb) on November 12. *I'm very relieved and happy that things went as well as they did considering all the incredible events which led up to the concert,* she said. She discussed photos a bit, then closed on an optimistic note. *I'm quite sure that by fall I will have more news for you, the way things are happening. My two major invitations are from "the Island Concert Hall series" in Long Island (this is for 1979-80 — too late for the coming season which includes Sills, Ashkenazy, Berman, Menuhin, etc.!) and the 92nd St. Y. Series (also 1979-80) in N.Y. — both very prestigious. Must go. Off to Florida with Bill and the kids on Monday. Love Sheila.*

There was a definite neglect of her in home town Toronto, despite the New York review and the two offers mentioned in her letter — apathy, lack of interest. There was no notice taken in the local media; national magazines such as Chatelaine seemed to ignore the fact that there was a career woman, par excellence, with more than a little glamour, worthy of an article. The CBC-TV Music Camera series were not interested in her, and the St. Lawrence Centre refused a suggestion that the New York concert be reproduced on their stage.

In fact, within the CBC, which had before sponsored so many of her efforts, doors were closing for Sheila, especially now that John Peter Lee Roberts, who had arranged for her recording of the Healey Willan Concerto, had left the network to head the International Music Centre. Srul Glick was still at the CBC, but in contrast to the past when he could readily arrange broadcasts for Sheila as well as recordings, now he couldn't do anything for her. He tried on so many occasions to get money for CBC recitals for her but was rejected every time. Sheila who could at one time arrange recitals for herself, ran into brick walls. The CBC's prime interest was in producing concert recitals by younger performers still "on their way up". She tried to arrange another concert with the TSO at Ontario Place, similar to the one she had performed with Fiedler. This, too, did not materialize. In one of her little 'notes to myself', she summed up 1978.

> The year 1978 has come and gone, as all other years, and became a link in the endless chain. Although it has been satisfying in a way, it hardly compensated for the frustrations and disappointments I endured. In many ways it has been unkind to me, and so were some of my artist friends. I feel that I have been deceived by those whom I trusted most. It's sad to realize that a certain amount of jealousy exists, even in art itself.
>
> Some artists are very egoistic and will seek fame even at the cost of undermining the dignity of a friend.

Louise Henig, Sheila's younger sister, is a stylishly attractive brunette whose artistic inclinations leaned towards dancing and playing the flute. Today she manages a successful high-fashion store on St. Clair Avenue West in the heart of Toronto's 'Little Italy'.

She remembers the end of '78, beginning of '79 well, as does Sheila's close friend, Carolyn Leslie, who was in the original cast of "Jacques Brel is Alive and Well and Living in Paris," both in New York and Toronto.

"Sheila's three most outstanding qualities," Louise remarked, "were her great kindness, her dedication to perfection and her art, and the way she felt so intensely about everything." Louise remembers Sheila's attention to her mother as she lay paralyzed at home year after year following her stroke. "Since my mother took ill Sheila had been, through the years, the catalyst of the family — a pillar of strength. She took on a mother image and cared very much about all of us. She treated my father like he was her own son." Concerning her dedication, Louise described Sheila as being "a perfectionist in an imperfect world". She was striving to be always perfect." This characterized not only her performances and her choice of programming, but the elegance of her home and the exquisite taste reflected in fashion, jewelry and lifestyle in general. Always exceptionally well-dressed, she had a very stylish and erudite taste in clothes. Always immaculately groomed, she demanded the same of her children. "She was like a walking fashion-plate," is how one of her friends described her.

Louise agrees — the perfectionism went beyond the piano; she feels that Sheila's compulsive cleanliness and immaculate personal grooming was an

Louise Henig Levy, Sheila's sister.

extension of her striving to be always perfect. She greatly admired Sheila's self-discipline, but on the other hand — "Sheila never had any fun in her life." Carolyn agreed: "Sheila was a very warm human being, a great giver. She received much less than she gave. If her taste wasn't yours — she wouldn't be offended. That was her way. And, she would talk so fast! I wouldn't get on the phone with her unless I had a lot of time." Srul Glick remembers that of Sheila also — and its probably put down (it's not uncommon amongst serious musicians) to the fact that the life of a concert musician is a lonely one, consisting mostly of practicing. It is not an uncommon trait, as if they are 'making up for lost time'.

"She felt everything had to rest on her shoulders," Louise said, "but she liked it that way. It was a fulfilled desire to feel needed. She couldn't ever take a back seat — with the choir, preparing for her concerts, whatever it was."

According to her family, she was crazy about animals. She threw away all of her fur coats and openly campaigned against the seal hunt. She tried hard to balance her life between the rigours and fierce dedication to music, and the warm home life which she craved, probably as a counter-balance to the exciting but uncertain life of a concert artist. She followed the Toronto Argos until, with their steady propencity to finish last, even diehard fans had trouble keeping faith. She and Bill installed a swimming pool, Sheila took swimming lessons. Family was, to Sheila, the necessary, natural, sturdy-like reliable skeleton of consistency from which to further develop her concert pianist career. She would never sacrifice the vital routine of family life, although, at times, she wondered to herself whether or not she would eventually have to do so.

> As the years go by I realize more and more that a performer cannot really be devoted to both stage and family, since it is impossible to do justice to the two, although the priorities may be equally important. As a result, one or the other may suffer. I don't think you can be completely dedicated to music while at the same time, carrying the responsibility of family life. And I think this probably applies only to female performers.
>
> On the other side of the ledger, however, I realize that I have given much pleasure and joy to thousands of people through my concerts and recordings, whom I have been able to reach with a universal language: this certainly makes it all worthwhile.
>
> I suppose everything is relative! I, too, have derived great joy and happiness from performing. It is a feeling of gratification that one cannot really define. It's a special kind of satisfaction which only an artist feels. Should an artist quit performing, there is nothing in his or her life that can take its place.

True, family life was very dear to Sheila. It was in the final analysis, the necessary structure, firm and durable from which her soul could soar as an artist. But — Louise summed it up: "Concerts kept Sheila happy. She really thrived on concert tours. When there was a lapse of concerts, she felt depressed, as most creative artists do."

Sometime, probably during the end of 1978 or early '79, Sheila started a letter, "Dear . . .", and then scratched it out. Instead she just wrote a couple of little paragraphs.

> *When you are unhappy, your thoughts go back to your childhood and the people you loved. Episodes and experiences of the past flash before your eyes which makes you sad and depressed. Your mind wanders back over a span of years that carried a heart full of hope and a promise of happiness and security, and you begin asking yourself some questions: "Have you wasted most of the precious years of your life by constantly helping and giving of yourself to those who were in need of assistance? I feel that I have derived a lot of satisfaction by being able to help, even though I am now repaid in an unkind manner, which naturally adds to my depressed state of mind, and I wonder if my efforts were justified.*
>
> *However, I find some consolation when I think back and recount all the joys and inner satisfaction I derived from sharing and giving. Then I believe that it was all worth it.*
>
> *I practice several hours each day and find that music is the basis of my life, and can be an antidote to unhappiness.*

May of '79 was unseasonably warm for that time of year, but nevertheless welcome after the winter. On May 15th, 1979, early in the morning, Sheila Henig was found slumped over the wheel of the family car, in the garage, dead from carbon monoxide poisoning.

Her father, as best he can, has tried to reconstruct those last few days.

"She had called me on Friday evening and told me that she was going to do a concert out of town on Saturday night, May 12th, and would be back home on Sunday. As Shawna's birthday was coming up she mentioned briefly the injury she had sustained on Shawna's birthday the year before, when she twisted and broke her ankle on the rug in the living room, and for two months was hobbling around with a cast on her foot. 'This year,' she said, 'I am not making a party at home. We'll take her and some of her friends out for dinner on Tuesday, [the 15th]. I have some beautiful gifts for her — I hope they'll please her. I still can't believe that she is already fourteen years old; the years have flown past so quickly.'

"She called on Sunday afternoon to tell me all about the performance. She seemed relatively happy with it. 'I played very well, considering the poor orchestra they had', she said. She was in high spirits and pleased to be at home.

"On Monday, the 14th, I was working on my novel and couldn't decide on the proper phrasing of a paragraph. I decided to consult Sheila and ask her opinion. It was about 3 p.m., the sun was shining, and the day was warm and pleasant. She answered the phone, sounding out of breath. 'Why are you puffing so heavily?' I asked. 'I was in the pool practicing my breast stroke,' she laughed, then added, 'but I don't think I'm ready to compete in the swim across the lake [Ontario] this year.' I then read the paragraph to her and asked her if she thought it was grammatically correct. She didn't seem to grasp its meaning at first and asked me to read it over again, she said she'd been distracted by a dog barking. I read it over again, and she agreed it was correct.

"She then proceeded to tell me about the arrangements for the following day.

" 'I am going to the hairdresser at 10 a.m., I'll have lunch with a friend of mine after that, and then we'll all go out for dinner together in the evening. Louise will pick you up.'

"I was somewhat uneasy when I hung up the phone, thinking that it's not like her to ask me to repeat a phrase, since she was always so quick and definite in her replies to any queries of this nature I had asked before. But then, I thought, perhaps she was just tired. I tried to dismiss the concern that bothered me.

Mr. Henig stopped for a moment, and then continued. "That evening, I did something quite unusual for me. I hardly ever went to concerts —except to Sheila's — since my wife had taken sick so long ago. I loved them, but it was something I shared with my wife, it had been an important part of our life. At any rate, I had two tickets for a concert at the Beth Sholom Synagogue for that night, Monday night. I remember telling Sheila I had them and, of course, wouldn't be going. She was quite adamant — 'You've been living like a hermit all these years. Go to the concert, you've got to try and go out once in a while.' So I went. I'm sure the music was fine, very enjoyable, but I was very nervous, I didn't want to be there. It is difficult to describe the feeling, I was uneasy, on pins and needles, obsessed with anxiety and worry and there seemed no reason for it. At any rate, I certainly didn't enjoy the concert and the minute the last number was finished I rushed out and went home. I don't think I've ever experienced a feeling like that in my life before. I know I grabbed the phone to call Sheila the minute I got in, then looked at the clock and put it down. It was close to eleven o'clock and I didn't want to disturb them. If she was tired she might be in bed. I took my coat off and the next thing I knew I had the phone in my hand again. Again, I put it down. I decided I would call her first thing in the morning. Now, of course, it seems much clearer —premonitions, whatever you want to call them — but I can barely live with the feeling I could have perhaps prevented this tragedy.

"Tuesday morning was dark and depressing. It was raining when I had some breakfast and decided I was not in the mood to go to the office. Rather, I went back to bed.

"Some time later, my housekeeper called me downstairs, saying there were some people here to see me.

"I came down and saw Bill leaning against a door in the living room. His father and his brother-in-law were sitting down with their heads bowed low, and Bill's mother was curled up in a corner of the room crying uncontrollably. My first thought was that someone had been in a car accident. Without looking up, Bill murmured three devastating words to me:

'Sheila is dead.'

"For a minute I couldn't comprehend what he said. And then it was as though the whole world had collapsed — I don't mean that as a cliche, the whole world did collapse. I was sinking into oblivion, a terrifying sensation gripped my mind, my whole body. I hung on to the stairway railing desperately while the house was spinning around me. The feeling was fear, almost of terror. Bill was saying something and I couldn't hear him, but slowly I realized more fully what had happened and that it was a terrible, terrible tragedy.

"I was taken into their car and driven to Sheila's home which was packed with people. There was a lot of food on tables, drinks, and some of the people there were even drunk by this time. I looked around me and thought that there was a party in progress, but how ironic and how unfair that the hostess wasn't there. My immediate impressions were wrong, I think, it wasn't a party, but it seemed people were talking terribly loud — 'Why am I here?' I thought, in an irrational sort of way. Some people were talking to me but I couldn't understand a word they were saying. Everything was devastatingly unbelievable and impossible, nothing was making any sense. I slumped into a chair, and to me, nothing seemed to matter any more. I was glad when total shock took over and blotted out my existence.

"I was taken to the Temple, and there was a tape of Sheila's latest recording being played. Every note dropped like a sharp, stabbing pain. I could swear I saw Sheila sitting there playing, but I was completely oblivious to what was actually going on. There's a time lapse in there, I know, but I don't remember any details. For so many days afterwards, it seemed that I would 'come to' for brief periods of time and find myself in another location or with other people. I couldn't recall how I got there.

"There are so many thoughts that go through your mind — many of them don't make sense. For instance, the obituaries, and the papers certainly covered her death. It was impossible for me to accept that this woman, my daughter, an artist, who had had hundreds of reviews and interviews in her lifetime was no longer here, and was not aware of the announcements the media carried which represent the finale.

"And the eulogies at the funeral service, at Temple Emanu-El. Rabbi Bielfeld said wonderful lovely things about Sheila, but they were things I knew so well, anyway. 'She was a genius, an artist of international fame . . . she had a heart of gold. She was compassionate and forever she was helping others.'

Mr. Henig asked that a poem be included. Sheila had actually drawn it to his attention at one time, remarking that it had been recited as an eulogy for someone's funeral — she thought it was a very beautiful tribute — but for Harry Henig it expresses better than he could himself, his continuing feeling of Sheila's presence, the endless remembering.

> At the rising of the sun and its going down,
> we remember her.
> At the opening of the buds and the rebirth of spring,
> we remember her.
> At the rustling of the leaves and in the beauty of the autumn,
> we remember her.
> When we are weary and in need of strength,
> we remember her.
> When we have joy we crave to share,
> we remember her.
> When we have achievements based on her's,
> we remember her.

"When we hear a piano playing classical music, we remember her," Mr. Henig added. Then he mentioned, "I did write a eulogy of sorts, for myself, which gave me a bit of peace. I think it summed up, organized in a strange sort of way, my rampaging feelings at the time."

> The music room is now quiet. The piano is standing in gloomy silence, mourning the loss it has sustained. Only echoes of brilliant classical music played in the past can be heard faintly, when one's mind wanders back to happier days before tragedy ended this artist's brilliant career in the prime of her life. Posters and reviews from the international music world that tell of success and fame are still covering all the walls. They, too, look wilted and saddened in the unbearable vacuum created and suspended in the deafening silence of this once pulsating music room.

"Then, of course," he continued, "the months pass and you think and think and there is no answer — there just isn't any answer at all!"

The remembering again is very difficult for Mr. Henig. He is still trying to solve that awful puzzle of "why?".

The immediate question, "why?" is unanswerable, as it is in such cases, although there is, in hindsight often hints to half-answers. In the case of Sheila it is more than usually perplexing because she was a giant in the Canadian music world and internationally recognized and renowned. She was extraordinarily intelligent, and presumably her capacity to take pleasure in herself could sustain her through most setbacks or depression-causing events which fate might put in her way. She had a comfortable existence in her Bayview home with its swimming pool, a husband and two very attractive children, plus a menagerie of pets.

For her father, it was a shock from which he will never fully recover; to her colleagues, a perplexing mystery, even amongst those who understood the often volatile, tautly-strung nature of the performing artist. To the outsider, it is mysterious because from the day she was born, her life seemed paved with the golden aura of success and achievement.

PART V
Epilogue

Harry Henig, 1975

Epilogue

Sheila's good friends, the Lugsdins from Winnipeg, wrote Bill and the children a long, deeply shocked letter extending sympathy and remembrances of Sheila's performances and her extraordinary loyalty to old friends. They mentioned that CBC Winnipeg had paid a tribute to Sheila just before the morning news and that Ann Lugsdin had been interviewed, about Sheila, on the program.

In May, 1979, one of Sheila's most loyal professional friends, Lou Applebaum, was putting together the proposed Healey Willan retrospective show for CBC-TV. The proposed taping date was to be September 21, 1979. There was no question Sheila would have been the performer of the Willan Piano Concerto. The show was in the preliminary stages, the script itself had not yet been written. Because nothing had been finished, Lou felt that he could not, in all due conscience, tell Sheila anything about these plans. And so Sheila knew nothing.

There were other plans nearing finalization. A few days after Sheila's death her friend Carolyn Leslie met Nicholas Goldschmidt on a plane to New York and he told her about the plans that were just about completed for the Healey Willan centennial year celebration. Sheila had been chosen to perform with the Toronto Symphony Orchestra (it was to be either Maple Leaf Gardens or the O'Keefe Centre). Goldschmidt was going to call Sheila in a few days, when he returned from New York. Carolyn told Mr. Henig that she told Goldschmidt, "It's too late", and Goldschmidt sadly concurred. In fact, the planned Willan centennial was never held, for Sheila was the essential performer in the celebration.

There is a sadness and sense of futility in recounting these things, for the question always comes up — if she had known, would her death have taken place. But these questions are only symbolic of a symptom, they are not the core question, which is, why was it so difficult for Sheila Henig to get meaningful work, consistantly enough, as an artist in Canada. Why was a woman of such undisputed gifts not a figure of reknown and national respect in her own country?

It is not an isolated incident. Milton Barnes, who knew Sheila well and had worked with her often, said when asked this question, particularly in relation to Sheila's death: "There but for the grace of God go I and a line up down to Bloor Street." He was standing on the corner of Lowther and Brunswick at the time and the question made him angry.

Many of Sheila's colleagues and friends acknowledge the question, and try to answer it, but the answers lie in the realm of blame and 'what-ifs'.

"The words that come to me are, 'such a waste'," replied Srul Glick. "It's the great Canadian tragedy; there is very little for them here. Canada just doesn't have the population to support the arts."

Yet, taking this demographic factor into account, Canada has a network of publicly-subsidized arts foundations and organizations from the Canada Council to the CBC to the National Ballet to the Canadian Opera Company to provincial parallel organizations, which the United States, for instance, doesn't have, in order to provide for a cultural scene which does not have to depend exclusively on the marketplace in a country beset by small population and large inter-city distances.

John Roberts, who is now the Past-President of the International Music Council, affiliated with UNESCO and therefore has an international perspective of the music scene, felt part of Sheila's problem was caused because, "there are not enough opportunities in Canada for performers. Canada cannot have a viable musical life with only activities in a few large cities — we need more touring possibilities. In Canada we seem to have become too concerned with the star system. The problem is that other countries can more easily back up emerging artists with recordings and effective promotional machinery. Therefore they are able to line up engagements almost anywhere in the world for their artists. This had meant that Canadians have tended to very often value foreign artists more than the struggling home-grown variety. Sheila was trying to forge ahead when this situation was probably at its worst."

Mr. Roberts broke off for a moment to pay his own personal tribute to Sheila as an artist. "What made Sheila unique was her real insight into the romantic repertoire; she always brought strong and interesting viewpoints to bear on this music; her performances were always compelling and her playing had a sense of freshness about it; the music sounded reborn — if I can put it that way . . . For me her performance of the *Sonata in B Minor* by Liszt was extraordinarily interesting because she had something very individual to say with it. I for one get very tired of run-of-the-mill performances of the standard repertoire by performers who have good technical equipment and not much more.

"Ironically," Mr. Roberts continued, again on the central theme, "for a variety of reasons, nowadays more Canadian performers are being used on major series than ever before and at last we seem to be experiencing an upswing of interest in Canadian performers."

Concerning Sheila's problems in dealing with the mass media, Roberts said, "The broadcasting industry here in Canada was greatly complicated because of the arrival of cable and we have ended up with a programming-spread so deficient in Canadian content of real substance that it looks like an expansion of the American networks — at least a lot of the time. The CRTC has had enormous difficulty in bringing order and reason into the broadcasting explosion in Canada and some people go so far as to say we have unwittingly sold our cultural birthright to others. In the vast number of radio and television channels available only the CBC has acted as the beleagured cornerstone for Canadian programming. (More than 95% of its radio music budget is spent on Canadians.) The overwhelming influence of foreign programming in the programming-spread has done something to shape Canadian attitudes. For example, apart from those who over-emphasize performers from other countries, it is not unusual to find Canadian students who feel that foreign professors must be better than those on home ground. Again, if we do launch a successful cultural venture in Canada, we begin to be worried by its success and go into a negative tailspin about it."

While Mr. Roberts insists that there must be a balance of use of foreign talent in relationship to home talent development, he clearly states that, "Without outlets on home-ground, the scene here will stultify." Simply put, it means we must promote home-grown talent, at *home,* more.

The question then, he suggests, should be, "What is preventing the CBC and other government arts agencies from developing unified and integrated policies which would balance better the importing of foreign artists?

"It is a complex one, as we are talking about balancing better the use of Canadian artists with those from elsewhere. It is not a question of excluding foreign artists because if we want Canadian artists invited overseas their foreign counterparts must be able to perform here. I repeat, it is a matter of arriving at a more equitable balance. The CRTC, the CBC and the Canada Council have all worried a great deal about Canadian content as have other departments and agencies. If the policies of the cultural elements in Canadian life are not integrated, it is because there is no real mechanism to allow this to happen. The situation is further complicated because of the involvement of the provinces in all the arts and one would have to say that the private sector of society also has major responsibilities and a real role to play in this area too. In short, with so many different elements now at work, one can only describe the cultural scene as fractured. Certainly it has not always been easy for artists to deal with all the segments of the cultural mosaic — particularly in the past."

Milton Barnes has a query along the same lines. "How is the artist, who is basically alone, he's not attached to any organization, supposed to find out who supports what, if the agencies themselves, with all their administrative tentacles and setups, don't know what the other is doing? It is unfair that the unsalaried artist should have to spend his time researching what agency does what for whom, then invest his time and the time of fellow artists to draw up their proposals and applications according to the administrative needs of these agencies. Because, for sure, without our applications, these people wouldn't have jobs."

Mr. Barnes knows from experience, exactly how much time and collaboration is involved in such applications. "If it's turned down, you never know why, and you never know what they chose in place of your collective proposal."

While Mr. Henig understands Mr. Roberts' logic and expertise, he himself feels that most of the blame lies with the CBC. "It should be the major performing and publicity vehicle for classical music. The CBC isn't dependent upon ratings, it's strictly non-commercial and it could accommodate *generously* all of Canada's serious music performers such as Sheila, throughout their careers. It should be a high quality classical music network." While Mr. Roberts recognizes the good intentions here, he points out that the CBC operates according to the Broadcasting Act, "and if you read the Act you will see that it's impossible for the CBC to do this and fulfill the mandate required of it."

Mr. Henig is not alone in his beliefs, for there are other people concerned with classical music who agree with him — Mal Thompson (who produced Sheila's *Piano Portraits*), Walter Babiak and Carolyn Gundy for a few. They feel that, in the past, the CBC has done just that — when Sheila was beginning her career, in the '50s and '60s, there was far more classical music programming than there is now, and it was on the AM network, where it had national coverage, as opposed to the present, where the bulk (according to Mr. Henig) of the classical music programming is placed on the six or seven FM stations which can be heard only within a 50-mile radius of the country's largest cities.

CBC-TV is even in worse straits, Mr. Henig maintains. "Chamber music recitals which featured, in the past, such regular performers of classical music as Sheila and Carolyn Gundy, are now replaced in prime evening time by top-40 survey-pop programs like "Ninety Minutes with a Bullet". The shift in emphasis at the CBC came during the late 1960's when the controlling powers, so afraid of what they perceived as 'British classical colonialism' decided to be 'with it' and instead exchanged it for a form of American pop-colonialism disguised as Canadian pop-nationalism which would leave cosmopolitan classical music distinctly out in the cold."

In any question of this nature, the CBC gets a lot of flack. But the media gets even more. "The press was much more classical-music oriented then (in the 50s and early 60s) than it is now," states Walter Babiak, a further example of what Mr. Henig calls the "slavish attempt to be trendy". The accusation goes out that the media has de-emphasized classical music per se and has thus decreased public demand for it out of sheer lack of promotion on the more basic levels. Mal Thompson heartily shares this opinion; he remembers his years with the broadcast industry in Britain where the *BBC Radio Times,* through its authoritative, informative coverage and background of the music being performed greatly aroused public enthusiasm in all segments of society for classical music throughout Britain. This, Mal feels, is desparately needed on a mass promotional basis by the CBC. But looking on a larger, everyday scale, Mal is highly condemnatory towards the general press for woefully underexposing classical music. "There is far too much emphasis on the 'trendy' and 'way out' (as exemplified by the Toronto *Star's* "Street Talk" and the Globe and Mail's "Fanfare" sections) which gives the current pop-music trends front-page fullcover treatment because they happen to be appearing in one of the bars in town. The classical music soloist rarely receives this treatment for a major concert." Mal Thompson very frequently ran into untold frustrations in trying to get classical, or even middle-of-the-road albums reviewed by the Toronto daily press. "It's almost as though there is a conscious plot to ignore some of the most vital parts of a performer's career."

Lou Applebaum supports Mal Thompson's position regarding press coverage of classical music. "News coverage of the classical music scene in Toronto is totally inadequate. We really don't have a stimulating journalistic environment."

Although the press seems to believe that youth is not interested in classical music, hundreds of high schoolers line up for the TSO student concerts and tickets for solo performances by classical performers. All the major high schools in Toronto boast student orchestras playing classical and light-classical repertoire. CFRB still programs its 'Starlight Serenade' of light classical music in prime evening time. CHFI has an all-night 'Music till Dawn' classical music program, hosted by De B. Holly, who was dropped from his former CBC-FM morning program slot in favour of a more 'popular' youth-oriented approach, encapsulating what one musician refers to as being the "isolation of the press from the actual cultural life of Toronto today."

And there is the 'anti-star' syndrome. "The Canadian trait is to keep everything on the same mundane level. There is a fear of excellence," says Stuart Hamilton. The media and the CBC will encourage new young prodigies, such as the young pianist Louis Lortie who at the age of 19 has already played with the Toronto Symphony.

"Once you're an established artist," says David Zafer, "a mature professional, it becomes dreadfully difficult." He also added, "Had Sheila travelled more, she would have had a career." But she had travelled sufficiently enough to certainly establish her mark on the world's leading music centres.

This 'anti-star' syndrome results in what Lou Applebaum terms the cyclical reputations of all Canadian serious music performers. They ascend. They reach a peak of popularity for a few seasons at a relatively young age. And then they pass out of "fashion" for a while, maybe to enjoy a resurgence of public-media popularity at some later time. Among pianists who have been affected by this cycle pattern, besides Sheila, are Ronald Turini, Marek Jablonski and Arthur Ozolins.

There are those who knew Sheila, such as David Zafer, who attribute much of Sheila's later professional difficulties to what he terms a "dreadful lack of management". Sheila herself, on the only Toronto-TV interview she ever did (Brian Linehan's *City Lights*), perhaps out of professional despair, attributed a successful career as being primarily a matter of business and publicity, specifically referring to the youthful career of Louis Lortie. In part, this is true, but Sheila herself enjoyed much the same hoopla when she was his age.

Stuart Hamilton believes that the prevailing attitudes of the majority of the Toronto newspaper cultural critics "has had a very negative influence", and indeed, Toronto has consistantly enjoyed the reputation of having the meanest critics of any major North American city, not only for its own performers but also for international celebrities. Walter Susskind was not, by any means, the only major cultural figure who received negative reviews in Toronto which he received nowhere else; there are many who received the same treatment, to the point where they refuse to perform in Toronto. They include such household names as Sammy Davis Jr. Among Canadian-born stars who made it to the top and who won't perform in Toronto are Rich Little and opera tenor Jon Vickers (personal interview with Stuart Hamilton, Nov. 20/79).

If Sheila received "bad notices" in Toronto (as she did with her first performance with TSO of the Dvorak Concerto) she also received 'sluff-off' indifference, ultimately more damaging to a performer's career. The best that the Toronto press could come up with after two acclaimed tours of Europe was something about sticky piano keys and shovelling wood and a recounting of her coughing fit in Rotterdam. The underlying intent seemed to be the deflating of the 'glamour image' down to the level of the mundane 'plain-folks' from which, according to the anti-star syndrome, she had the impudence from which to rise in the first place. After 1960, when she had passed the "promising" stage, she never received the rave reviews in the Toronto press she had received elsewhere, with the exception, perhaps, of some of George Kidd's articles.

Stuart Hamilton had a few strong remarks concerning the general attitude of critical negativism to the 'keep-everything-on-the-same-'level' anti-star mentality and fear of excellence. He attributes the real beginning of this attitude to the CBC-TV program, *Tabloid,* in the early sixties, which encouraged a fashionable negativism, ostensibly for the sake of "anti-establishment" controversy but actually promoting a rude common-folk anti-elitism masked by what he terms an "immature irresponsibility". "By putting everything down," Hamilton declares, "it makes them, the critics, look like they're on top. I have, for some time, objected to the parochialism of the critics in Toronto. I feel that anyone can write a bad review, but it takes someone with perception and talent to write a fair review."

Only very recently, according to Hamilton, the Toronto serious music critics seem to have lost some of their vituperation, although he believes that they still lack the all-important inherently positive approach which is so necessary to build up and to sustain a healthy serious music scene.

This attitude of the Toronto critics, that is, their lack of a fundamentally constructive approach, was echoed by many of the musicians who worked with Sheila and knew her well. Chris Clark, Sheila's page-turner, states that the Toronto critics tend to criticize on a personal rather than on a professional level. Walter Babiak also makes mention of the mechanical "put-down" mentality of the press and their prosaic "anti-highbrow" approach. Stanley Solomon, as permanent a fixture in Toronto's classical music world as is possible, also castigated the Toronto media attitude as being: "if it comes from Toronto it has to be lousy". He also agreed that the critics must be much more constructive and much more encouraging of the truly great local Toronto scene, which, as a seasoned veteran who has regularly performed in all the major musical centres, he readily recognizes has consistently produced musicians of top world-stature calibre. "For solo classical singers and instrumentalists," says Stuart Hamilton, "the last ten years have been bad."

Walter Babiak

Gordon Kushner

Stuart Hamilton

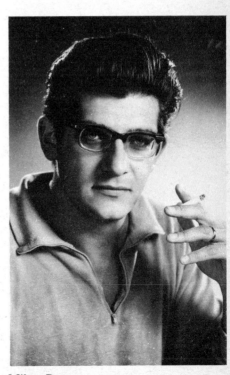

Milton Barnes

Louis Applebaum

John Peter Lee Roberts

What is more important than any of these remarks, perhaps, is what Sheila herself had to say — *In Canada a female classical concert pianist unfortunately does not stand a chance. If you were a Japanese, English, Swedish, American, Russian or Israeli, you would have a much better opportunity of exposure than being a Canadian. I refuse to accept the theory that it is a kind of female persecution. I think it is a simple inferiority complex on the part of those hard-core individuals who control your destiny on the concert stage.*

This book about Sheila Henig has tried to trace the achievements and accolades garnered by her during her lifetime; this was the easy part for they are well documented here and abroad and if you add them all up and place them end-to-end, it is a staggering — a wonderful — record. To trace or probe or analyze the emotional makeup of this lively, nervous and enormously gifted woman is difficult to impossible for nobody realizes that the possibility of an early death exists while they are in the midst of living a life and signposts are not noted. A character appraisal from one person will be refuted or changed or embellished upon by another, which only serves to remind us we are all different things to different people. Only little clues exist and these are only useful to give insight into the character of a many-faceted individual. They do not serve as a "reason" or even as a psychological base for post-mortem purposes.

William Littler in the Toronto *Star*, December 20, 1980, writes from an objective viewpoint, tinged with subjectivity, about another "treasurehouse", the album that Sheila and Daniel Domb recorded in 1977, and he conjectures on the reasons for Sheila's death. In the final analysis, that is all anybody can do because her act was a definitive one, but also a private one.

REQUIEM TO A PIANIST
Grieg: Sonata for Cello and piano in A minor;
Glick: Prayer and Dance. Ginastera: Pampeana
No. 2. Falla: Suite Populaire Espagnole.
Daniel Domb, cello, with Sheila Henig, piano. CBC SM348.
   It is difficult to listen to this album without mixed feelings: feelings of happiness in response to the splendid music making it contains; feelings of sadness accompanying the awareness that this duo will never make music again.
   Daniel Domb is, of course, still very much with us, having recently given recitals in Toronto and New York between his regular duties as principal cellist of the Toronto Symphony. There isn't a finer cellist in Canada than this native of Haifa and graduate of Juilliard.
   But Sheila Henig is no longer with us. She was found last year, slumped over the steering wheel of her fume-filled car, having apparently taken her own life. Her death at the tragically early age of 44 remains a mystery.
   If there is a clue to the mystery it may be found in the biographical notes accompanying this valedictory recording, for the notes describe a career full of promise that somehow petered out.

After winning the Eaton Award in 1955 as the most promising graduate student from the University of Toronto's Faculty of Music, she went on to become a Laureate of the Geneva International Competition and one of the best known young pianists in the country.

But as the years passed, other young pianists came along and Sheila Henig, lacking energetic management and the right breaks, treaded water. She played a little, taught a little, even became a fellow panelist with yours truly on the CBC radio program, Music and Opinion.

Then, in 1978, she made one last effort to secure an international career by presenting a daring Evening of Music at New York's Carnegie Recital Hall, both playing the piano and singing. It came off. The New York Times published a complimentary review and back to Toronto flew a jubilant Henig, ready to answer the inevitable phone calls.

But the phone didn't ring. Oh, she did get one or two engagements as a result of the New York recital, but that was about all. She couldn't even persuade Toronto Arts Productions to let her repeat the Evening of Music under their auspices.

What this blow did to her morale we can only guess. What we know is that a fine artist has left this CBC disc as a memorial. As Daniel Domb remarks: "We had a unique musical and personal communication which lent a special glow to all our rehearsals and concerts. Sheila always brought such warmth and artistry to our sessions, making those musical moments forever unforgettable."

The actual recording was made in Timothy Eaton Memorial Church, with Keith Horner as producer and Ed Marshall as audio technician. The balance unnecessarily favours the cello but the sound is otherwise quite satisfactory. The performances are more than that.

The recording is available only by mail, by writing CBC Merchandising, Box 500, Station A, Toronto M5W 1E6. The price is $8.98 plus tax."
Nothing has changed, only the price is higher.

* * * * * * * * * * * * * * *

Canada Council awarded a first prize for the best recording by Canadian artists Daniel Domb and Sheila Henig in 1980.

December 15th, 1978.

I am sitting in my music room, looking at posters, reviews and other material in various languages from many parts of the world. I suddenly realize how much time and effort I have given over the years to accumulate these headlines. All of my life I have been obsessed with an uncontrollable urge to perform, to create and to achieve something that only a very few have been able to accomplish, although my rewards have, in a way, surpassed my expectations in the world of music. Nevertheless, it just doesn't seem enough for me. Something within me stirs and urges me on to achieve even greater heights, or did I perhaps set my sights too high and I didn't accomplish what I had hoped I would? I am always trying to reach for a star, because I believe that it's better to reach and miss, than not to reach at all.

Sheila Henig, from her diary.

Sheila Henig in her music room.